Fun with Nature

TAKE-ALONG GUIDE

Caterpillars, Bugs and Butterflies
by Mel Boring

Frogs, Toads and Turtles
by Diane L. Burns

Rabbits, Squirrels and Chipmunks
by Mel Boring

Snakes, Salamanders and Lizards
by Diane L. Burns

Tracks, Scats and Signs
by Leslie Dendy

Trees, Leaves and Bark
by Diane L. Burns

illustrations by Linda Garrow

NORTHWORD PRESS
Minnetonka, Minnesota

CREATIVE
PUBLISHING
international

NorthWord Press
5900 Green Oak Drive
Minnetonka, MN 55343
1-800-328-3895

Library of Congress Cataloging-in-Publication Data

Boring, Mel,
    Fun with nature / by Mel Boring, Diane L. Burns, Leslie Dandy;
illustrations by Linda Garrow.
      p.   cm. -- (Take-along guide)
  Includes index.
  Summary: Provides detailed descriptions and illustrations of more
than 150 different animals and plants.
    ISBN 1-55971-684-3 (pbk.). -- ISBN 1-55971-702-5 (hard cover)
    1. Natural history--Juvenile literature.   2. Nature study–
–Juvenile literature.   [1. Nature study.]   I. Burns, Diane L.
II. Dendy, Leslie A.   III. Garrow, Linda, ill.
IV. Title. V. Series.
QH48.B7824   1998
508--dc21   98-31913

Printed in Malaysia
10 9 8 7 6 5

Contents

Caterpillars, Bugs and Butterflies

DEDICATION
For Zack, my son and research assistant, with love.

ACKNOWLEDGMENTS
A book is never made by one person, and I want to thank two special people among the many who helped me make this one. Thank you Dr. Orley R. "Chip" Taylor of the University of Kansas Entomology Department and his Monarch Watch program for helping me get to know caterpillars and butterflies like friends. Thank you, Dr. Barbara Stay of the University of Iowa Department of Biological Sciences for showing me how bugs and caterpillars and butterflies are all close cousins.

Contents
Frogs, Toads and Turtles

DEDICATION
To Clint and Andy, who have had these creatures in hand at one time or another.
Pass along the wonder.

ACKNOWLEDGMENTS
Special thanks to Jim and Kirsten Kranz and Dawn Bassuener, whose knowledge, expertise in the field, and patience in answering my many questions are greatly appreciated.

Contents

Snakes, Salamanders and Lizards

DEDICATION

For today's children, who are tomorrow's herpetologists.
Save room in your world for untamed creatures.

ACKNOWLEDGMENTS

Grateful thanks to my brother, and sister-in-law, Jim and Kirsten, who generously emptied their library
on behalf of my research and answered countless questions. Also, my husband, Phil, for additional
herpetological knowledge and especially for ongoing support and patience.

Contents

Rabbits, Squirrels and Chipmunks

DEDICATION
To my mother, Helen Tuthill, who first taught me love,
and taught me to love all living creatures.

ACKNOWLEDGMENTS
Librarians help make books, and this book was no exception.
My special thanks to Bob Lane, of the University of Iowa Biology Library, for his help.

Contents

Tracks, Scats and Signs

DEDICATION

To my father, the scientist, whose curiosity is still contagious.
And to my mother, the artist, who saw beauty in every blossom and beaver.

ACKNOWLEDGMENTS

Much of the information in this book is based on the expert knowledge of wildlife scientists with lifetimes of tracking experience. The adult tracking books of Olaus J. Murie, Paul Rezendes, Chris Stall, Louise Richardson Forrest, and Preben Bang are highly recommended to anyone who gets hooked on tracking and wants to learn more.

I would like to thank my husband and children for their help and encouragement on my own fact-finding field trips. Blair and Laura Swartz generously donated bear scat and squirrel nibblings from their yard.

The library staff at University of New Mexico-Los Alamos provided a never-ending stream of interlibrary loan materials and enthusiasm. And Barbara Harold at NorthWord Press helped me see the forest through all the trees.

Contents

Trees, Leaves and Bark

DEDICATION

To today's children, who care for tomorrow's trees.

"I love all trees . . . "

—Aldo Leopold (naturalist)

ACKNOWLEDGMENTS

"The woods are lovely, dark and deep . . ."

—Robert Frost (poet)

And lovely also are the people who helped prepare this manuscript:
The staff of the Rhinelander District Library, D.N.R. forester Mike Beaufeaux, U.S. Forest Service silviculturist Dick Cutler, Dot Heintz and the UW-Extension 4-H program in Oneida County.
Special thanks to: Dan Krueger, Jr., professional horticulturist from Northwoods Nursery, for his expertise.
Consolidated Paper Company forester Dan Hartman, for his knowledge, patience, and meticulous help.

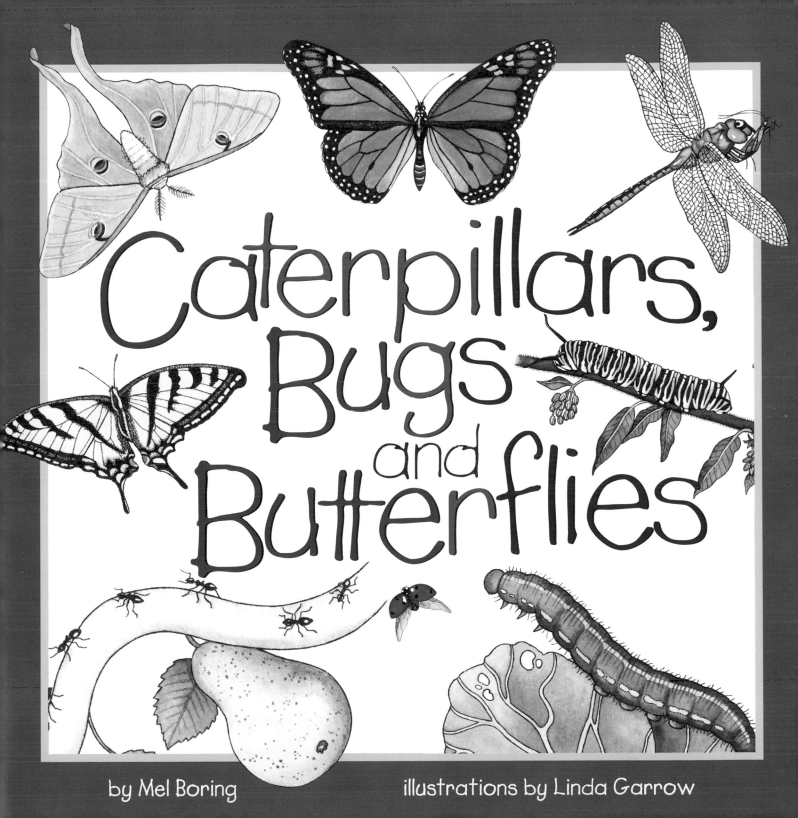

Caterpillars, Bugs and Butterflies

by Mel Boring   illustrations by Linda Garrow

INTRODUCTION

Caterpillars and bugs and butterflies are all members of one big "family"—the insects. Most of the time, we just call them all bugs. But how could they all be from the same family? They don't look alike at all. The little black ant looks as different from the huge cecropia moth as a mouse from an elephant.

All caterpillars, bugs and butterflies have one thing in common: CHANGE. The changing they do is easiest to see when a caterpillar becomes a butterfly. That is a complete change, from one creature to another. It makes them totally different creatures. This change is called metamorphosis.

A bug like the grasshopper is changing all the time, too. A grasshopper nymph "child" has a short body and legs that look too big for it. As it grows, its body slowly becomes longer and sleeker. And it grows wings for flying. These changes happen little by little.

This Take-Along Guide and its activities will help you know about the many stages of insect life. Nymph, grub, pupa, larva, cocoon, chrysalis and more. You can use the ruler on the back cover to measure what you find. You can use the scrapbook to draw what you see.

Have fun exploring the amazing world of Caterpillars, Bugs and Butterflies!

CATERPILLARS

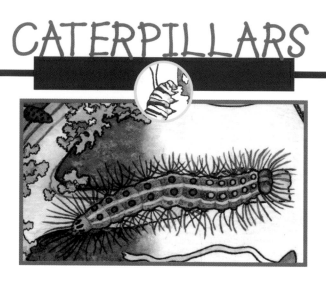

The caterpillar that crawls out of its egg is called a larva. It can only crawl about three feet a minute, so it hides from enemies on the bottoms of leaves. That's where you will find most caterpillars. A larva eats nonstop for about a month. It outgrows its skin and bursts through it several times as it grows. When a larva pops out of its last skin, it becomes a pupa.

The pupa stage is a short "rest stop" before it becomes an adult. Pupas don't eat, they just rest. Maybe they're saving up energy to fly.

The complete change from larva to adult happens while it is a pupa. When a butterfly caterpillar sheds its last skin, its inner skin hardens into a chrysalis. A moth caterpillar doesn't make a chrysalis. It makes a cocoon. First, it hooks a silk strand to the top of twig. Next, it fastens that same thread to the bottom of the twig. Then it hangs head-down and spins threads across for the rest of the cocoon.

Find a chrysalis or cocoon and watch the new butterfly or moth emerge!

CABBAGE BUTTERFLY CATERPILLAR

What It Looks Like

The cabbage caterpillar is green or tan. Its skinny body grows no longer than your thumb. It looks like a tiny cucumber, so it can easily hide on a plant, and is hard to find. It is the first bug of spring, and can be found in any garden cabbage patch.

What It Eats

The cabbage caterpillar was named for its favorite food. It also eats broccoli, cauliflower and radishes. And it likes mustard plants and some flowers. It is covered with velvety fuzz.

The yellow-billed cuckoo is one of few birds that eat this caterpillar. Other birds don't like to eat such a fuzzy meal.

On quiet days, if there are many cabbage caterpillars attacking a cabbage patch, you can actually hear them chewing!

Where to Find It

Look closely to find this caterpillar because it will be hiding its skinny body behind a fat leaf or a thin stem. In the woods, you will find cabbage caterpillars where trees are not too close together. They also like the open space of a farm field. And of course, look in cabbage patches.

MONARCH BUTTERFLY CATERPILLAR

What It Looks Like

Here's a caterpillar that looks like a little candy stick. Its white, yellow and black rings might look like peppermint, lemon and licorice to you. But to birds and other enemies, they are colors of DANGER, telling sparrows, chickadees and blue jays to keep away.

This caterpillar is about the size of your middle finger, and it can squeeze shorter or longer like an accordion.

What It Eats

The monarch caterpillar eats mostly milkweed. That bitter-tasting weed makes it taste terrible, because milkweed contains natural poisons. They don't harm the caterpillar, but they make its enemies sick. So hardly anything eats this caterpillar.

Where to Find It

You can see the monarch butterfly caterpillar from April through September. It lives in open areas like meadows and fields, and on roadsides—wherever milkweeds grow.

Its egg is smaller than a pinhead. Yet, in the first two weeks of its life, the monarch caterpillar grows to 2,700 times its birth-size. An 8-pound human baby growing at the same rate would weigh over 10 TONS at two weeks old!

TIGER SWALLOWTAIL CATERPILLAR

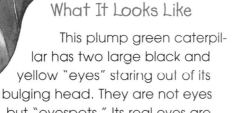

What It Looks Like

This plump green caterpillar has two large black and yellow "eyes" staring out of its bulging head. They are not eyes that see, but "eyespots." Its real eyes are smaller. They are on its head, too, in front of and below the eyespots.

If its scary-looking eyespots don't frighten birds away, the tiger swallowtail raises its red "stink gun." It is a Y-shaped "horn" found behind its head. It oozes bad-smelling goo to drive enemies away.

What It Eats

You can look for the tiger swallowtail caterpillar on a wide variety of trees and shrubs. It eats leaves from mid May to mid July.

Where to Find It

This caterpillar rests on a pad of its own silk all day, with a leaf curled around it like a blanket. It comes out at night to eat. It grows about as long as your middle finger.

Over winter, this caterpillar can be found in its pupa, among the litter on the ground, or on one of the trees it feeds on. It will look like an orange-brown piece of bark, with a silk thread holding it around the middle.

MOURNING CLOAK CATERPILLAR

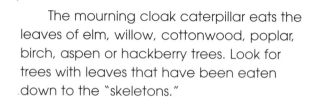

What It Looks Like

The mourning cloak caterpillar is black with white speckles and a row of red diamonds on its back with black bristles. It has shiny eyes. It grows about as long as your ring finger.

When this caterpillar becomes a butterfly, its wings are mostly dark-colored, like old-fashioned funeral shawls worn by women. That is how they got the name "mourning cloak."

What It Eats

The mourning cloak caterpillar eats the leaves of elm, willow, cottonwood, poplar, birch, aspen or hackberry trees. Look for trees with leaves that have been eaten down to the "skeletons."

Where to Find It

Mourning cloak caterpillars can be found in open woodlands, and along riverbanks and forest edges. They gang up in groups big enough to strip all the leaves off young trees. They are easy to find in June and July.

Young mourning cloak caterpillars hang out together in webs. If you disturb their web, they wiggle like dancers dancing.

GYPSY MOTH CATERPILLAR

What It Looks Like

Gypsy moth caterpillars look like tiny parade floats. They are decorated with twelve bright red dots and ten blue dots down their backs. There are tufts of brown bristles along the sides of their bodies. The gypsy caterpillar grows about as long as your index finger.

What It Eats

These caterpillars always seem to be hungry. They eat the leaves of 400 kinds of trees—even pine tree needles. Every seven to ten years, from May to mid July, there is an outbreak of gypsy caterpillars in the Northeast, where most of them live. In their last big outbreak, they gobbled the leaves off 13 million acres of trees and shrubs.

Where to Find It

Look for gypsy moth caterpillars on the ground during the day. They eat in trees all night, but by day, they drop down into litter around the tree.

In its 8-week lifetime during the first half of summer, one caterpillar can eat a whole square yard of leaves. Assassin bugs eat gypsy moth caterpillars.

BANDED WOOLLYBEAR

What It Looks Like

The banded woolly-bear caterpillar is easiest to find in autumn. By then it has a wide brown stripe around its middle and black on both ends. This thumb-sized caterpillar rolls up into a ball when disturbed.

Some people say the woollybear can forecast the weather. The more black it has, legend says, the colder the winter will be. But scientists say it grows less black as it gets older. So a woollybear with more black is really just a younger caterpillar.

What It Eats

The woollybear eats garden plants and clover in the summer. Its enemies are mostly birds. But most birds don't like such fuzzy food, so they don't eat too many.

Where to Find It

In fall you will see it crawling out of gardens, over lawns, even across highways. In spring, the woollybear caterpillar spins its cocoon out of its body hair and silk. It becomes the isabella moth, a member of the tiger moth family. So, the "bear" turns into a "tiger."

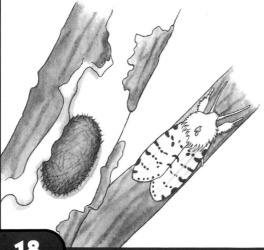

CECROPIA MOTH CATERPILLAR

What It Looks Like

The cecropia caterpillar looks kind of scary. It has a row of dinosaur-like spikes down its back. The front ones look like clubs with knobs on the ends. Cecropia caterpillars are apple-green.

What It Eats

This giant caterpillar uses its huge mouth parts to find food, since it is nearly blind. It has strong senses of touch and taste.

Where to Find It

Cecropia eggs are laid in the spring on elm, willow, ash or lilac trees. But as this caterpillar grows, it may move to a greater variety of trees and shrubs.

Look for its tough, brown or gray, big-bag cocoon firmly attached to a twig. The cocoon is easily found in winter when trees are bare. Sometimes you might find the cecropia making its pupa in the ground, instead of in a cocoon on a tree. Cecropia caterpillars become cecropia moths in the spring.

TOMATO HORNWORM

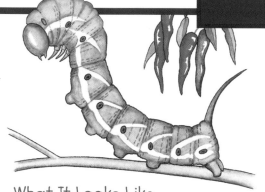

What It Looks Like

The tomato hornworm's rear "horn" looks frightening. This caterpillar rears its head back as if it wants to fight when you touch it. People think it stings or is poisonous, but it is not. In fact, its scary "horn" is soft, and not harmful at all.

The tomato hornworm is green, with a row of yellow arrowheads along each side pointing toward its head.

What It Eats

Tomato hornworms gobble up the leaves of tomato plants, and sometimes the tomato itself. Tomato hornworms also eat the leaves of peppers, eggplants and weeds. You will see them in summer in the garden.

Where to Find It

Birds are the main enemies of this caterpillar. But it makes a tiny squeak to frighten them away. It also hides on plants. The arrowheads on its sides look like leaf veins, so it probably doesn't look very tasty to enemies.

When it is a month old, and longer than the width of your hand, the tomato hornworm lowers itself to the soil on a silk thread and buries itself underground. Out comes the sphinx moth in spring.

CAPTURE A "BEAR" FOR THE WINTER

The woolly bear caterpillar isn't really a bear. And it is as tame as a teddy bear. So capture it for the winter, then watch it spin its cocoon in the spring—and then turn into the isabella tiger moth!

WHAT TO DO

1 Find a brown and black banded woolly bear caterpillar in October, crawling across the lawn or garden.

2 Put it in a clear plastic collecting jar with holes in the lid.

3 Put a twig or two in the jar, and some fresh green grass for it to eat. Put fresh grass in every day. It will perch on the twig for a few days or a week. Then it will lie down to sleep on the bottom.

4 Carefully take out any remaining grass, but leave the twigs in the jar all winter long.

5 Keep it in a place outside that is protected from bad weather. You will be able to watch it hibernate.

6 In spring, when weeds start to turn green outside, the woolly bear will need food. Feed it fresh grass every day, Then watch it spin its "magic" cocoon of silk and hair.

7 In a week or so, it will become the isabella tiger moth. On a nice day, take the moth outside and set the "tiger" free.

BUGS

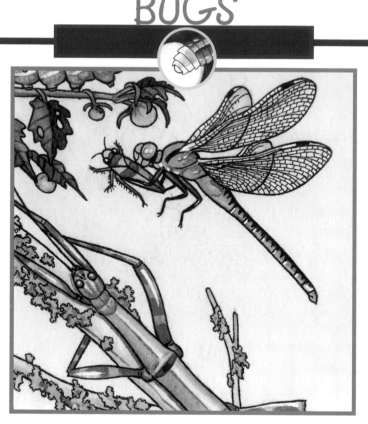

The baby bug that hops out of its egg is called a nymph. Nymphs look a lot like the adults they will become in two or three months. Nymphs are fast hoppers—from plant to ground and back, unlike most caterpillars that stay put on their plants.

Nymphs eat a lot! Some eat as much as 16 times their weight each day. That would be like you eating 930 pounds of food every day. Nymphs outgrow and shed their skin many times before they become adults.

All true bugs have an "X" on their back. The crossing of their wings or wing covers make the "X." One wing overlaps the other when the bug is resting. You can see that the milkweed bug is a true bug by its red "X." But the June bug has no "X." It is born a larva, called a grub. It spends its life underground until it becomes an adult.

See how many true bugs you can find!

LITTLE BLACK ANT

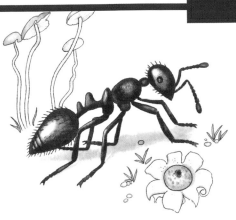

What It Looks Like

There are 10,000,000,000,000,000—that's ten million billion—ants in the world! In fact, there are more ants than all the rest of the insects put together. One little black ant is only half as big as a grain of rice.

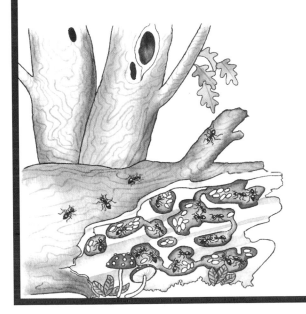

What It Eats

Ants eat other insects and fruit, and whatever crumbs they can find. Frogs, birds, spiders and other insects eat ants.

Ants "talk" to each other using scent signals. When a little black ant finds a crumb, it hauls it back to the nest. And it leaves a scent trail from its bottom. Other ants will follow the trail to find more crumbs. If you rub your finger across the scent trail ants make, the ant parade will stop. You rubbed away the smell that led them to the food.

Where to Find It

Little black ants live everywhere, but usually near trees. Most ants are female. No ant lives alone, and all ants share their work. In winter, they move down to the deepest levels of the anthill. But in cold winter places, ants hibernate.

TRUE KATYDID

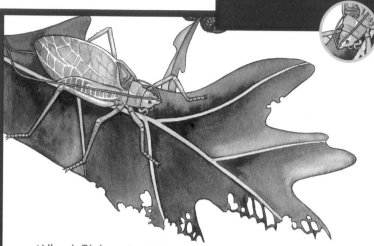

What It Looks Like

What insect says its own name? The katydid. It sounds like it is arguing with itself: "Katy did, Katy didn't, Katy did." It is hard to see Katydids, but if one is around you will surely hear it. Katydids grow about as long as your first finger. Each katydid has long antennae that run back and curl under its bottom.

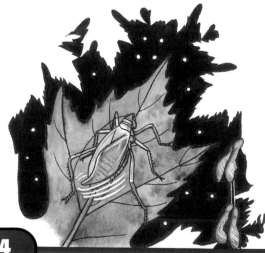

What It Eats

Katydids are as green as the leaves they eat. Oak, maple, apple and cherry trees, and shrubs are their favorites. They hide from birds during the day by looking like leaves. At night bats eat them.

Where to Find It

Katydids lay eggs in the fall on the loose bark of trees, and on leaf stems. Katydid nymphs hatch in the spring without their wings. They grow them as they become adults.

The male katydid makes a special call at night. One of his wings is like a violin and the other is like a bow. He rubs one wing over the other, playing a love song that is heard by female katydids up to one mile away.

FIREFLY

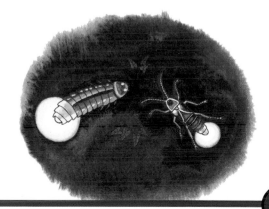

What It Eats

Most fireflies eat nothing because their lives are so short. Those that do, eat pollen, nectar and other soft-body insects.

Where to Find It

Fireflies use their lights to attract a mate. You can see them find each other on your lawn or in an open field, after sunset in June through August.

The firefly's enemies don't seem to be afraid of its light. In fact, sometime you may find a frog with a light glowing in its tummy. It is not an alien—it just swallowed a firefly!

What It Looks Like

This bug is also known by other names like lightning bug and glowworm. But it is really a beetle—with lights. When full-grown, the firefly is almost as long as the width of your thumb. Its wing covers are blackish-brown, with dull yellow borders. Female fireflies do not fly.

Even the larva of the firefly glows. The glow makes light but not heat. Oxygen mixes with body fluids in the firefly's tail and makes "cold light." The firefly turns its light on by sending oxygen to its tail, and stops the oxygen to turn it off.

JUNE BUG

What It Looks Like

The June bug is the "tank" of the insect world. It is built like a stout box, and can grow to be nearly as long as your nose.

When June bugs fly, they look like double-wing airplanes, with wingcases held high so their flight wings can move freely. Their legs and antennae are spread out like radar.

Where to Find It

Its name could be "May beetle" because it is really a beetle, and you often see it in late May. By June, you will hear it before you see it—buzzing against your open window screens. It is reddish-brown and oval-shaped. If you hold your magnifying glass over its antennae, they look like tiny moose antlers.

What It Eats

When you see the buzzy bug, it is already two or three years old. Most of that time it was a grub or larva, curled up like a plump "C" underground, eating the roots of trees and shrubs. This gray-white grub likes to eat corn, potato, onion and strawberry roots even better. Birds, skunks and pigs like to eat June bug grubs.

FIELD CRICKET

What It Eats

Crickets eat other insects, including each other, and dead animal remains. And they eat plants like tomatoes, peas and beans. Mammals, reptiles and spiders eat crickets. But their worst enemies are birds.

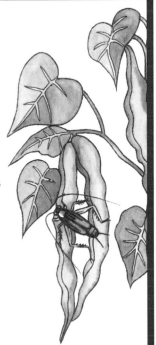

What It Looks Like

The field cricket is about the size of your eye. Its head is as wide as its body, and the antennae reach down past its bottom. Field crickets are black, with red-brown stripes on their wing covers. They have short wings.

Crickets have wings that "sing" by rubbing against each other. A cricket can be a "ventriloquist," lowering its "voice" when you are near, to make it sound far away. But look close around you, it may be right at your feet!

Where to Find It

Adult crickets appear by July and August. Look for the field cricket on your lawn, in fields and woods, as well as along roadsides—wherever you hear them chirping. Check under things for them, too, such as rocks and logs.

LATERAL LEAFHOPPER

What It Eats

Leafhoppers stab their dagger beaks into a plant's sap stream like vampires. As leafhoppers go from leaf to leaf, they leave behind a sweet-tasting liquid called "honeydew." Flies, bees and wasps like to eat it. They eat leafhoppers, too. So do sparrows.

What It Looks Like

Most leafhoppers are smaller than your little fingertip. A lateral leafhopper is black with brown stripes making a "V" between its wings. Its body is slender and oval. It has a stabbing "beak" used to sip plant juices. The beak is under the head.

"Lateral" means "sideways," and lateral leafhoppers have the unusual ability to run sideways. Leafhoppers are called "dodgers" too. When the plants they are on are disturbed, adult leafhoppers hop or fly away sideways, and duck under the leaf. So always turn the leaves over very carefully.

Where to Find It

Lateral leafhoppers are easiest to find in June, July and August because by then they are full grown. You will find them on weeds and grasses, flowers (especially asters) and trees—nearly everywhere.

LADYBIRD BEETLE

What It Looks Like

You probably know this beetle by another name: Ladybug. It can fly. And of course, not all ladybugs are ladies—some are males. The ladybug is the world's favorite bug. In some parts of Germany, the ladybug, and not the stork, is said to bring newborn babies.

This shiny, round bug comes in different colors: red, orange, yellow, brown, tan or gray. It may have polka dots or stripes. Some have as many as 22 spots. And some have no spots at all. But most ladybugs have black spots on red or orange wing covers.

What It Eats

Aphids are a ladybug's favorite food. They also eat leafhoppers, mites and other small insects.

No bug eats ladybugs, because they squirt stinky goo from their knees. The goo is poisonous, but only to other bugs.

Where to Find It

You will find ladybird beetles in your garden, on flowers, grapes, apples, potatoes or corn.

AMERICAN BIRD GRASSHOPPER

Grasshoppers have powerful legs, which are spiny and scratchy. Some people say grasshoppers spit tobacco juice. It is really harmless, brown stomach juice. They spit when they are picked up, to defend themselves. It probably tastes yucky to bird enemies.

What It Eats

Grasshoppers eat grass of all kinds. They eat plants that grow in the spring. They also eat tree leaves.

What It Looks Like

Grasshoppers are vanishing experts. Some grasshoppers just hop or jump, but the American bird grasshopper flies, almost as well as a bird. Its main colors are brown and tan, with a yellow stripe down its back. They grow to be about as long as large paper clips.

Where to Find It

You will find American bird grasshoppers zooming around fields, meadows and forest edges. It is nearly everywhere, June to August.

If you could hop as well as a grasshopper, when you play baseball you could jump from home plate to first base—90 feet!

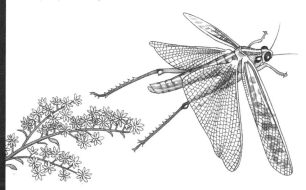

MILKWEED BUG

What It Looks Like

The milkweed bug is named for the plants it eats. Milkweed bugs are oval-shaped, and no longer than the width of your finger. They lay eggs on milkweed plants when the leaves and flowers come out in spring.

The milkweed bug has "warning colors" to show its enemies it is poisonous to eat. Some bugs have warning colors, but are not poisonous. But bright orange monarch butterflies, red-orange ladybugs, and red milkweed bugs are poisonous to eat, and flash like "stop lights" to their enemies.

What It Eats

They eat and live on milkweeds all summer until the first frost. Then they dive into leaf litter, logs, or into houses, and hibernate over winter.

Where to Find It

This bug is sluggish and slow. It usually flies straight with no tricky twists, so it is not hard for birds and spiders to catch. That is why it does not fly unless it has to, but stays hidden under leaves. Look for it wherever there are a lot of milkweeds.

PERIODICAL CICADA

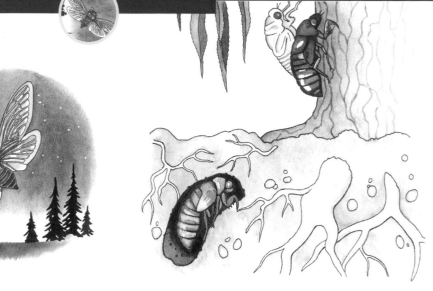

What It Looks Like

The periodical cicada is black or brown, about an inch long, with bulging, glowing red eyes and see-through wings. Look for it in July and August. It may look fierce, but it doesn't bite or sting.

Periodical cicadas spend either 13 or 17 years growing underground. Then the nymphs climb up the nearest tree or post, and shed their skin. Adults live only 40 to 60 days. If your life cycle was like the periodical cicada's, you would spend 71 years growing up!

What It Eats

Cicada nymphs suck juice from plant roots. Adult cicadas feast on tender tree twigs and leaves.

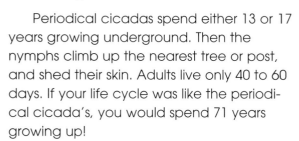

Where to Find It

The cicada's buzz sounds like a power saw cutting through metal. No other insect sounds like the cicada. The sounds come from the vibrations of the cicada's skin stretched over hollows on its body.

On summer evenings, you hear the cicada's "buzz saw." Find which trees the sounds came from, then look for the cicadas in daylight. Cicadas are hard to find, because they flatten themselves on the other side of a tree when they hear you coming—and then fly away fast.

NORTHERN WALKINGSTICK

What It Looks Like

Can sticks walk? Walkingstick insects can. But they only walk at night. In the daylight, they hold so still that they look exactly like little sticks with six legs. That is how they escape their bird enemies.

The northern walkingstick grows to be about as long as your first finger. Its relative, the giant walkingstick in the southern United States, grows to be almost six inches long. This walkingstick is the longest bug in the world.

Sometimes, a walkingstick's leg may break off. But it can grow new ones. The new legs are never as big or strong as the originals, but they still have six.

What It Eats

Walkingsticks spend nearly their entire lives sitting still, and chewing leaves around them. They eat locust, walnut, cherry and rose leaves. They especially like oak and hazelnut trees.

Where to Find It

Use a flashlight to find northern walkingsticks after dark. Look on the trees where they feed.

Since walkingsticks stay hidden by not moving, you might see one if you make it move. Shake a branch and watch the ground underneath it. You just might shake a "stick" off!

DRAGONFLY

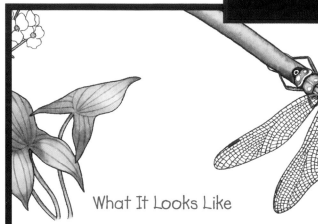

What It Eats

Other insects are its only food—and it will even eat other dragonflies. Dragonflies carry a "food basket" with them. They curl their six legs inward, forming a "basket" to carry away the food they snatch while flying—dragonfly "fast food."

What It Looks Like

The "dragon" of all bugs is the dragonfly. And it is one quick bug. It flies up to 35 miles per hour.

The dragonfly has been around for over 300 million years. Today's green darner dragonfly fits on your hand. But prehistoric dragonfly wings spread almost 2 feet across!

To spot its food, the dragonfly has the most powerful eyes of any bug. Most of its head is covered with its enormous eyes. It can see you move when you are still about 20 steps away from it.

Where to Find It

The most common dragonfly is the green darner. It is about as long as your middle finger. You will find it wherever there is a pond nearby. Look for it in August or September, on sunny days.

USE A "CRICKET THERMOMETER"

The warmer it is outside, the faster crickets chirp. You can figure out the temperature by counting cricket chirps and doing a little math.

```
  70° F
- 40 chirps
_____
  30 magic number
```

WHAT TO DO

1 To set up your "cricket thermometer" find out what the temperature is.

2 Listen to a cricket and count how many times it chirps in 15 seconds. Write that number down in the back of this book.

3 Subtract that number from the temperature.

4 This is the "magic number." For example, if the temperature was 70 degrees, and your cricket chirped 40 times, your magic number would be 30.

Now, you can figure out the temperature any time you want to. Just count the number of cricket chirps in 15 seconds and add your "magic number." The number you get is the temperature!

BUTTERFLIES AND MOTHS

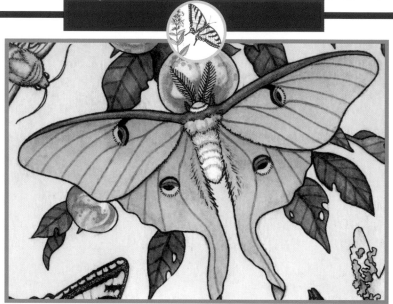

When a butterfly or moth breaks out of its chrysalis or cocoon, it is wrinkled and wet. It pumps body fluids into its wings until they unfold and dry. Then it can fly.

Moths spend the rest of their short lives looking for places to lay their eggs. Most of them do not even take time to eat.

Butterflies fly in the daytime, but most moths fly at night. Butterflies' bodies are slender. Moths have chubby bodies. Butterfly antennae are thin and smooth, with small knobs at the end. Moths have thick, feathery antennae. Antennae are their feelers and smellers. They use them to find food and mates.

An easy way to tell a butterfly from a moth is to watch it land: If its wings are folded together pointing up, it's probably a butterfly. If its wings are folded against its body or pointing out flat from its sides, it's probably a moth.

Butterflies and moths drink nectar with their proboscis—their tongue. It is long and curled up inside itself like a spring. They unroll this hollow tongue to sip the nectar—like you sip soda pop through a straw.

MONARCH BUTTERFLY

What It Looks Like

Monarch butterflies look "dressed up" for Halloween, in bright orange and black. From May until November, the butterfly you see most is the monarch.

It is easy to tell which monarchs are male. They have mating scent sacs on their back wings. Each has a tiny bulge on the black line at the center of the wing. These attract female monarchs.

What It Eats

You will find monarchs mostly on milkweeds. But they also sip nectar from lilacs, red clover, thistle and goldenrod.

Most birds don't eat monarchs because the milkweed they eat makes them poisonous to birds. It doesn't hurt the monarch but it makes birds sick.

Where to Find It

Look for monarchs flying through your yard, stopping to sip from garden flowers.

Monarchs are famous for migrating (going to a warmer place for winter). Most monarchs fly to Mexico. Some fly 2,500 miles in six weeks. Scientists have learned that they fly as fast as 35 miles an hour. One flew 265 miles in one day. That's how they got their nickname "wanderers."

TIGER SWALLOWTAIL BUTTERFLY

What It Looks Like

It has stripes like a tiger and tails like a bird! Bright yellow and black tiger swallowtails are high fliers, so look for them above your head. From spring to September, they soar among the tall tree branches. They may zip out of sight, then pop back suddenly.

A tiger swallowtail's wings can stretch from one end of a dollar bill to the other—about 6 inches. Their wing tails can be as long as one inch.

What It Eats

Swallowtails sail about in flight for hours at a time. They flit above flowers, pausing only to sip nectar from lilacs, phlox or honeysuckle. Even while sipping they keep their wings beating.

Where to Find It

Usually, swallowtails stay in groups. You will sometimes see them sipping from the edges of a puddle or stream. Male swallowtails also need the sodium in the water so they will be able to mate.

Sometimes you can smell the sweet smells male swallowtails give off to lure female swallowtails.

RED ADMIRAL BUTTERFLY

The red admiral has been known to land on the shoulders of gardeners who were in their gardens day after day. If you spend lots of time where red admirals are, one of them may put its admiral's stripes on your shoulder.

What It Eats

Juice from rotting fruit and tree sap are food for red admirals. They also drink the nectar of thistle, milkweed, dandelion, red clover, daisies, asters and butterfly bushes.

What It Looks Like

The red admiral got its name from its orange wing stripes. They look like the stripes admirals in the navy wear on their uniforms. They fly very rapidly and ziggy-zaggy. So red admirals are hard to see up close. A red admiral's wide open wings are about the length of your middle finger.

Where to Find It

Red admirals sail into gardens and fields, along the edges of woods and rivers, and in barnyards. Afternoon or evening is the best time to see one on porch roofs, or on shrubs or along sidewalks. At earlier, sunnier times, you will find them drinking from flowers or fruit.

CABBAGE BUTTERFLY

What It Eats

Cabbage butterflies like to eat what's in your garden, especially cabbages, radishes and nasturtium flowers.

The yellow on cabbage butterfly wings is poisonous to birds. That color comes from mustard plant flowers they sip nectar from.

Where to Find It

Some people don't appreciate the cabbage butterfly, because it is found so often—especially anywhere there is cabbage, and at almost anytime of the year except winter. It flies from the last frost of spring until the first frost of fall.

You can find cabbage butterflies in gardens, farm fields, open woodlands and cities. They are found around the flowers of mustard, milkweed, red clover, dandelion, dogbane, aster and lantana.

What It Looks Like

Cabbage butterfly wings are powdery-white on top and greenish-yellow on the bottom. The front wings have gray tips. Its wings spread only from about top to bottom of your little finger.

Cabbage butterflies have weak eyes. They may mistake a daisy for a mate if the flower is more than a foot away. They have a proboscis that is double-barreled.

Count the dots on a cabbage butterfly's wings: males have one, but females have two.

BUCKEYE BUTTERFLY

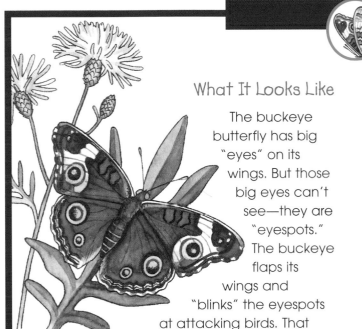

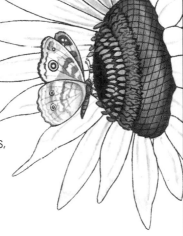

What It Looks Like

The buckeye butterfly has big "eyes" on its wings. But those big eyes can't see—they are "eyespots." The buckeye flaps its wings and "blinks" the eyespots at attacking birds. That shocks the birds for a split second, and gives the buckeye time to get away.

Buckeyes are very colorful butterflies. They have bright red bars on their front wings. Those bars and their "eyes" and their scalloped wing shape help you recognize buckeyes easily. Buckeye wings spread about the length of your ring finger.

What It Eats

Sometimes the buckeye sips from mud puddles. It also sips nectar from asters, sunflowers, peppermint, knapweed and milkweed.

Where to Find It

You might find a buckeye sitting on the ground, or beside the road on a sunny, hot day. It often pauses to bask in the sun with wings spread wide. You can find it in fields, meadows, or along roads from spring until fall.

Buckeyes play games of "air tag" with each other, and other butterflies. They even chase grasshoppers that are over twice as long as they are!

PAINTED LADY BUTTERFLY

What It Looks Like

Most butterflies look as if they were carefully painted with a brush. But the painted lady butterfly looks like the paint box was dumped out on it. On top, it is rose, orange and brown, with black and white "paint spatters." Underneath, it is pink, gray, orange and brown, spattered with white and black, and four bright eyespots.

Your ring finger will reach across the open wings of a painted lady.

What It Eats

Thistle flowers are the main places you will find the painted lady butterfly, sipping nectar. But also look for it on zinnia, cosmos, heliotrope, butterfly bush, mint, ironweed, red clover, milkweed and buttonbush.

Where to Find It

It flies wherever the land is open and bright, in gardens, parks, flowery meadows, deserts and mountains. Begin looking for this colorful butterfly in April, until fall's first frost.

Painted ladies are found in more parts of the world than any other butterfly. So painted ladies have many names, like "Cynthia of the thistle" and "painted beauty."

SILVER-SPOTTED SKIPPER

What It Eats

The skipper's long proboscis sips locust, iris, zinnia, honeysuckle, clover, and thistle nectar. Skippers hardly ever visit yellow flowers—scientists are not sure why.

What It Looks Like

Skippers seem to skip through the air, instead of just fly. That is why they are called skippers. The skipper is like a moth, and like a butterfly. The skipper rests with its back wings spread out like a moth, and its front wings up like a butterfly.

The silver-spotted skipper is the most common of the large skippers. Its wings can cover your middle finger's length. It is chocolate brown and has golden bands across the front wings. The back underwings have silvery patches, giving this skipper its colorful name.

Where to Find It

Look for skippers from May to September. They are in yards, gardens, open woodlands and along roadsides.

After all their skipping, skippers rest upside down, under large leaves. So they don't need protective coloring to guard them from hungry birds. Turn over a few leaves and see what skips out!

GYPSY MOTH

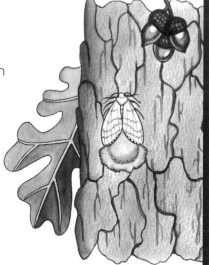

What It Eats

The gypsy moth does not eat anything during its one-week lifetime. It is as if it is living off energy from all the food it ate as a caterpillar.

What It Looks Like

One stormy night over a hundred years ago, the wind knocked over a cage of moths in Massachusetts. They had been brought from Europe. Some of them escaped. That is how the gypsy moth first got loose in the United States.

Gypsy moths have stout, hairy bodies. Males are brown with even darker brown markings. Females are white with brown marks. The male gypsy moth is smaller, too. Its body fits on a quarter. The female can spread her wings to the width of a dollar bill.

Where to Find It

You will find the gypsy moth in July and August, on pine and broadleaf trees, especially oak. They mate and lay their eggs on the trees.

Gypsy moths are day-fliers, unlike most moths. The male is a good flier, but the larger and heavier female just flutters along the ground. Gypsy moths have now spread as far south as West Virginia, and as far west as Minnesota and Texas.

CECROPIA MOTH

What It Eats

The cecropia moth does not eat. But you will find it on the same plants cecropia caterpillars eat: cherry, maple, willow, ash, and lilac. They rest at the base of trees, hidden on bark and dead leaves.

What It Looks Like

The cecropia may startle you with its color and size. Its wings are darker brown closer to the body, and striped with gold, orange and yellow. All four wings have white and red half-moon shapes on them. A cecropia's open wings reach from your wrist to your fingertips.

The male cecropia moth is smaller, with a more featherlike body. In mating, female cecropias send out "love scents" to male cecropias as far away as two miles. Up close, cecropia moths smell like peanut butter!

Where to Find It

Watch for them during May and June evenings on window screens or around a porch light. Cecropias also fly by day, unlike most other moths. They like open country, with trees and bushes.

LUNA MOTH

Male and female lunas look much the same. But the male has more feathery antennae. With them, he senses the female's mating perfume.

What It Looks Like

If you spot the spectacular luna moth, don't try to catch it. It is an endangered species.

The luna moth has very long tails. Its color is a glowing green, but it also has touches of purple, brown, yellow, white and gray. From wingtip to wingtip, it is a little shorter than your hand length. You may see it just beneath a streetlight, waggling its wings, as if dancing. When its long, dangling tails sway in the breeze, it looks like a little lunar-green "moon kite."

What It Eats

Luna moths have no mouths or stomachs. They do not eat, and only live about one week.

Where to Find It

As soon as the female comes out of the cocoon in April or June, she searches for a tree with leaves her offspring can eat. Many different trees could be food for her caterpillars. So you may find her on walnut, hickory, oak, birch, alder, sweet gum or persimmon trees.

MAKE "MOTH SUGAR"

Moths have antennae that look like miniature feathers. They work like radio aerials, picking up far-away signals. So they can scent "moth sugar" from miles away. Wait until late afternoon to spread "moth sugar," so the sun will cook but not evaporate it.

WHAT YOU NEED

- 3 tablespoons sugar
- water
- 1 quart plastic jug
- old paintbrush
- sponge

WHAT TO DO

1 Fill the jug with water.

2 Mix sugar into the jug of water.

3 Use the paint brush to brush the "moth sugar" on a stump, a rock, or a fence post. Or soak the sponge in the mixture and hang it on a tree.

4 Just after dark, go see your new visitors.

5 If no moths have come to the place, next time add a little apple juice to the "moth sugar."

There are more than 100,000 kinds of moths in the world—many will be attracted to this tasty treat!

something to do

SCRAPBOOK

Caterpillars, Bugs and Butterflies

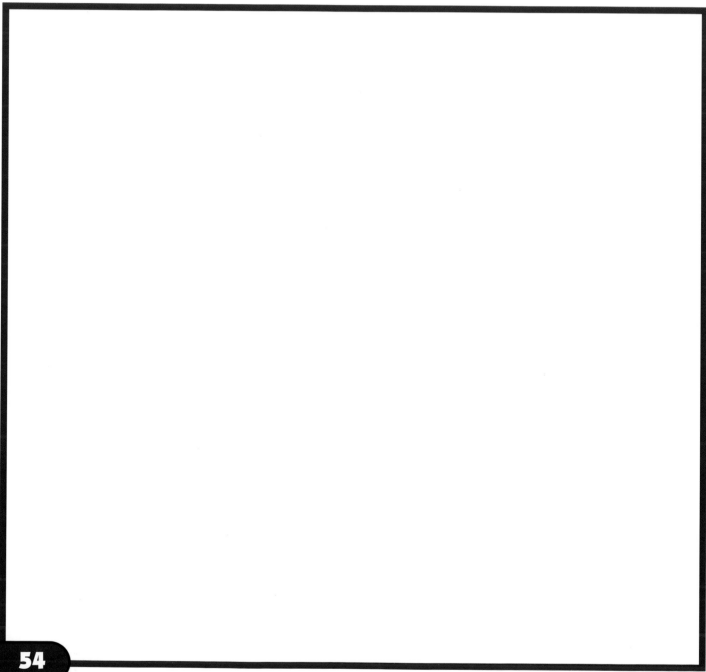

Frogs, Toads and Turtles

by Diane L. Burns   illustrations by Linda Garrow

INTRODUCTION

Frogs, toads and turtles are alike in some ways. All three are cold-blooded, which means their body temperature is the same as the air around them. To stay cool, they burrow underground or underwater. To warm up, they bask in the sun.

These animals all have four legs and a head, but no teeth. They don't have ears like people and some other animals have. Instead, they hear with an organ called a tympanum.

Frogs, toads and turtles are also different in some ways. Frogs and toads shed their skins as they grow, and most do not have a tail. A turtle does have a tail but does not shed its skin. And a turtle has a hard shell to protect it.

When turtle eggs hatch, little turtles come out. When frog and toad eggs hatch, tadpoles swim out. The tadpoles then turn into frogs or toads by metamorphosis.

Turtles stretch their long necks to help them see in all directions. Frogs and toads have bulgy eyes that can see all around them.

Frogs and toads "talk" by pulling air from the lungs into a vocal sac that makes the throat swell like a balloon. As the air travels past the vocal chords, it makes sound. A turtle can grunt or hiss, but it is much quieter than a frog or toad.

Have fun exploring the amazing world of Frogs, Toads and Turtles!

FROGS

Frogs are amphibians. They can live on land and in the water. Some are even found in trees. They are often together in groups.

Most frogs have sleek bodies with smooth skin. Rather than drinking through their mouths, frogs absorb water through their skin, which must be moist to keep them alive.

Frogs do not have ribs. They make soft landings on their chests when they leap. Frogs can jump longer than the length of their bodies. And for its size, a frog can swim 10 times faster than the fastest human swimmer.

There are several ways that frogs defend themselves from danger. They are slippery to catch and hold. They dive deep and stay underwater for long periods of time. They leap away from danger. Their skin color and markings help them to hide. Some may play dead. Others puff up to make themselves seem bigger.

BULLFROG

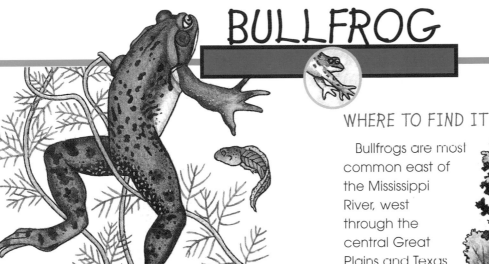

WHERE TO FIND IT

Bullfrogs are most common east of the Mississippi River, west through the central Great Plains and Texas and on the West Coast.

These frogs like wet places with shallow edges and overhanging brush, such as ponds, lakes and reservoirs.

On hot days, a bullfrog basks in shallow water with only its eyes showing. In winter, bullfrogs hibernate in the mud of riverbanks and lakes.

Their call is a deep, echoing croak: "*Chug-a-rumm*" and "*Knee-deep.*"

WHAT IT LOOKS LIKE

These frogs are wide and grow up to 7 inches long.

Their smooth, dull green to brown skin often has dark spots. The belly is whitish, sometimes with dark marks.

The back feet are webbed.

WHAT IT EATS

Bullfrogs feed at night. They eat mice, crayfish, salamanders, small birds, snakes, snails, crabs, fish, tadpoles and other frogs.

Don't hurry.
Take your time and have fun!

59

LEOPARD FROG

WHAT IT LOOKS LIKE

Leopard frogs are slender. They grow to be 2 to 4 inches long.

Their smooth skin is green or brown with dark, round spots. A green-yellow line runs from each eye down its back. Two ridges run down the middle of its back. The belly is yellow-white and may be spotted.

The leopard frog's back toes are webbed.

WHERE TO FIND IT

Leopard frogs are found throughout the United States except on the West Coast.

Leopard frogs live in groups along the wet edges of ponds, lakes and streams. They are also found in wet meadows when the grass is high.

During hot weather, they bask on lily pads. In winter, leopard frogs hibernate by burrowing into the bottoms of lakes and ponds.

Their short call sounds like fingers rubbing across a balloon.

WHAT IT EATS

This frog eats during dusk and nighttime. It likes spiders, wood lice, worms, flies and moths.

INTERESTING FACTS

This frog's name comes from the pattern of its skin.

Look for frogs in quiet, undisturbed water.

SPRING PEEPER

WHAT IT LOOKS LIKE

This small frog grows up to 1 1/2 inches long.

Its smooth skin is olive-green, tan or gray. Across its back is a marking that looks like an "X." The belly is reddish to yellowish.

Each toe has a tiny suction pad.

WHERE TO FIND IT

This treefrog is found everywhere east of the Mississippi River south to northern Florida, and west into Texas.

Spring peepers like the low edges of still, shallow water. They like woodland ponds, too. They cling to branches or blades of grass above the waterline.

Spring peepers hibernate under leaves and behind tree bark.

Their high trilling chorus sounds like jingle bells.

INTERESTING FACTS

The sound made by this tiny treefrog can carry as far as a half-mile!

WHAT IT EATS

Spring peepers eat at night. They like aphids, mosquitoes and small worms.

Use patience and sharp eyesight to find frogs.

CHORUS FROG

WHERE TO FIND IT

Chorus frogs are found from the Rocky Mountains, across the Great Plains to the East Coast, south to Georgia and west to Arizona.

This frog likes grassy edges of riverbanks, ponds and shallow swamps.

In cold places, they hibernate by burrowing under leaves.

Their raspy trill is especially noisy after a rainstorm.

WHAT IT LOOKS LIKE

Chorus frogs are slender with pointed snouts. They grow no more than 2 inches long.

Their smooth skin can be greenish-gray to brown. There is a dark stripe that starts at the mouth and goes through each eye. The belly is whitish and looks bumpy.

Some chorus frogs have dark, broken stripes down the back. Others have dark blotches or bright green spots rimmed with black.

Each toe has a small suction pad.

WHAT IT EATS

Chorus frogs eat mosquitoes and flies at dusk and nighttime.

Tell an adult where you are going, or take one with you.

CRICKET FROG

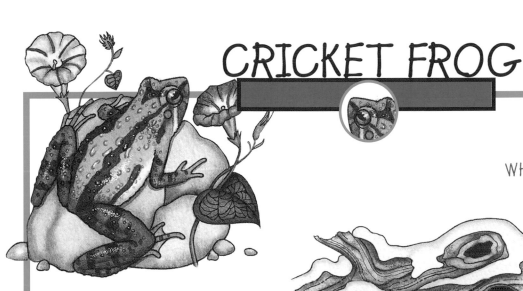

WHAT IT LOOKS LIKE

Cricket frogs are from 1/2 to 1 1/4 inches long.

They have rough, green or brown skin. Sometimes, there are darker reddish-brown markings on the back and legs. The belly is creamy. Some have a white stripe below the eye.

There is usually a red or green streak down the center of the back and a dark triangle shape on top of the head.

The cricket frog's back feet are webbed.

WHERE TO FIND IT

Cricket frogs are mostly found east of the Mississippi River.

Cricket frogs love shady places under leaves and overhanging branches around quiet pools and ponds.

In the cold north, they hibernate under leaves and logs.

The chorus frog's call sounds like two marbles tapped together. It goes faster and faster: *"Kick-kick-kick."*

WHAT IT EATS

Cricket frogs eat spiders, flies and aphids during the day.

INTERESTING FACTS

This frog's name comes from its insect-like chirp.

It lives on the ground and does not climb.

GREEN FROG

WHERE TO FIND IT

Green frogs are found east of the Mississippi River as far south as Florida and west to Texas.

They live along the edges of streams, springs, ponds and swamps.

Green frogs hibernate in winter, burrowing into stream banks and the bottoms of ponds.

Its call sounds like the twanging of a banjo string.

WHAT IT LOOKS LIKE

This chunky frog grows to be 2 to 4 inches long.

Its green or brown skin may be rough or smooth.

It has dark brown spots and blotches on the back and legs, and a ridge along each side of the back. The belly is white with dark spots. Male green frogs have a yellowish throat.

The back toes are webbed.

WHAT IT EATS

Green frogs eat at night. They like water insects, and also those flying just above the water's surface, such as dragonflies.

INTERESTING FACTS

This frog sometimes rests in shallow water, floating on its stomach with legs dangling down.

64

Don't chase frogs away from their homes.

WOOD FROG

WHAT IT LOOKS LIKE

Wood frogs grow from 1 1/2 to 3 inches long.

Their pinkish or brownish bodies are chunky. Their legs are long. The belly is lighter than the body.

A dark stripe with white edges runs from the eye along each side of the back. The eyes look like they have a dark mask across them.

The wood frog's back toes are webbed.

WHERE TO FIND IT

Wood frogs live in the North into Alaska. They are also found in the eastern United States, west as far as Wisconsin and into the southeastern mountains.

They like wet woods and grasslands, near water, but usually not in it.

During hot weather, wood frogs hide beneath fallen leaves and logs. They hibernate in winter beneath stones and logs.

They call from woodland ponds, just before late-winter ice melts. Their call sounds like "Kraack-arrack."

WHAT IT EATS

Wood frogs eat worms, insects and snails during the day.

Sit quietly away from the water's edge to see frogs.

PACIFIC TREEFROG

WHAT IT LOOKS LIKE

Pacific treefrogs grow to be 1 to 2 inches long. They have slender heads.

Their rough-skinned body is mossy gray, green or brown, often with darker spots. The belly is whitish.

A dark stripe runs from the nose and through each eye to the front legs.

This treefrog has sticky toe pads. Its back feet are slightly webbed.

WHERE TO FIND IT

Pacific treefrogs live along the West Coast from Washington to California, eastward into Montana, Idaho, Nevada, Utah and Arizona.

They are found on the ground or among plants at the edges of streams, ditches and ponds. They also live in burrows and rock crevices.

When very warm, they hide between the bark and wood of fallen tree trunks. They hibernate under stones and in logs and bark.

Its call is a musical, 2-note chorus, with the second note higher than the first: "*Kreck-ek, kreck-ek.*"

WHAT IT EATS

Pacific treefrogs eat flies, small worms, beetles and spiders at dusk and nighttime.

INTERESTING FACTS

This treefrog can change its body color to match what it is sitting on or near.

Be aware of everything around you.

GRAY TREEFROG

WHAT IT LOOKS LIKE

Gray Treefrogs are chunky. They have wide heads and grow to be 1 1/2 to 2 inches long.

Their rough, bumpy skin is gray or green with dark blotches on the back. They have a yellowish spot under each eye.

The belly is whitish or gray. The inside of the back legs is orange.

The toes have suction pads. The back feet are webbed.

WHAT IT EATS

At night, this frog eats the insects it finds in cracks and crevices of tree bark.

WHERE TO FIND IT

Gray treefrogs live in every state east of the Mississippi River. They live as far west as Minnesota, south through Kansas and into Texas.

They like open, shallow water with trees standing in it.

In cold places, they hibernate under tree bark.

Its musical trill sounds like a calling bird: "*Wit-wit-wit.*"

INTERESTING FACTS

Gray treefrogs live in trees almost their whole lives.

Their skin looks like tree bark with moss.

GREEN TREEFROG

This treefrog is nicknamed the "rain frog" because it often sings before a thunderstorm.

Green treefrogs like wet edges of swamps, ditches and ponds. Sometimes they can be found on lighted windows at night.

These frogs don't hibernate. They can be found all year long.

Its call often sounds like the "Quonk" of a cowbell.

WHAT IT LOOKS LIKE

Green treefrogs have smooth skin and pointed heads. They grow to be 1 1/2 to 2 1/4 inches long. Their slender bodies and legs may be bright green, gray-green or yellow.

A creamy stripe runs from the mouth along each side of its body. Sometimes, there are also tiny yellow-orange spots on the back.

The belly is yellow-white and bumpy.

Its toes have suction cups. The back feet are webbed.

WHERE TO FIND IT

It lives along the Atlantic Coast from New Jersey to Texas. It is also found in the South and along the Mississippi River as far north as Illinois.

WHAT IT EATS

Green treefrogs eat flies, mosquitoes and other insects.

Get permission before going onto someone's land.

MAKE A FROG PUZZLE

You can have a frog with you anytime you want, by making your own frog puzzle. Here's how:

WHAT YOU NEED

- A plain white piece of flat, stiff cardboard

- Fine-lined markers in a variety of colors or a box of crayons

- Scissors

- An empty shoe box

WHAT TO DO

1 Using the markers or crayons, draw your favorite frog on the cardboard. Make the drawing as large as you can without going off the edges. You can draw the frog hopping, sitting, eating, sleeping or swimming.

2 Color in the animal, including its spots, blotches and lines.

3 Using a marker or a crayon, draw squiggly lines all across the picture. Let the lines go in different directions and from edge to edge. (HINT: For an easy puzzle with big pieces, draw only a few lines far apart. For a harder puzzle, draw lots of lines close together).

4 Cut the picture apart into its puzzle pieces using the scissors.

Mix up all the pieces. Now you are ready to have fun putting your frog back together!

When you are finished playing with your puzzle, you can store the pieces in the shoe box.

TOADS

Toads are amphibians like frogs. But toads prefer dry land. They would rather be near water than in it. They are often found by themselves rather than in a group.

Their bodies are chubby and their skin is rough and bumpy. It is dry, not moist or slippery.

Toads have short, thick legs. They only hop distances shorter than the length of their bodies.

A toad's color helps it hide from enemies. Another toad defense is that their skin tastes bad to enemies that might try to eat them.

Some people think that you can get warts from toads, but that's not true. Toads don't even have warts, they just have bumps on their skin.

AMERICAN TOAD

WHERE TO FIND IT

American toads live in the eastern United States from New England south to Georgia, west to Oklahoma and north into Minnesota.

They like gardens and fields, and stay cool beneath woodpiles and stones.

They are more active at night than during the day. They hibernate in their burrows.

WHAT IT LOOKS LIKE

The American toad grows to be 2 to 4 inches long. It has a pudgy body. It has a large, blunt head and nose. Some have yellow throats.

The skin looks paint-splattered. It is brownish-green to red-brown, and may have a light stripe on the back. It often has large spots with bumps on the back. The light belly has smaller bumps.

There are often dark spots on its legs and sides.

Its call is a deep whistle lasting up to a half-minute: "*Burrrr . . .*"

WHAT IT EATS

This toad eats crickets, flies, locusts, sow bugs, worms and beetles.

Watch where you step.

EASTERN SPADEFOOT TOAD

WHAT IT LOOKS LIKE

This short, fat toad grows to be 2 to 2 1/2 inches long.

The smoothish, brown skin has a few bumps. It usually has 2 yellowish stripes down its back. The belly is grayish-white.

The short, thick legs have broad, webbed back feet. Each back foot has a "spade" on it that helps them dig their burrows.

WHERE TO FIND IT

Eastern spadefoot toads are found in sandy places along the Atlantic Coast from Massachusetts to Florida, and west to Texas. They also live down the Ohio River to Missouri and Arkansas.

They are active at night, especially after a heavy rain. They stay in their burrows during the day. They hibernate in cold northern areas.

Their short call is a harsh, crow-like "Whaarh!"

WHAT IT EATS

This toad eats flies, spiders and ants.

INTERESTING FACTS

This toad can absorb so much water through its skin that it swells like a little balloon.

SPECIAL WARNING

Do not touch spadefoot toads. They can make your skin burn.

GREAT PLAINS TOAD

WHERE TO FIND IT

This toad lives across the Great Plains from western Minnesota to the Rocky Mountains, south to Texas and across the Southwest into California.

It likes the edges of ditches and grassy river bottoms.

It is active usually at night, and burrows into the ground during the day. It hibernates in cold areas.

The piercing, low call sounds like a toy horn. It can last 20 seconds or more.

WHAT IT LOOKS LIKE

Great Plains toads are chubby and grow to be 2 to 4 inches long.

The gray-brown to green-yellow skin looks bumpy. Most have pairs of large, dark blotches with light edges. They usually have a creamy stripe on the back.

Young toads have a "V" marking between the eyes.

Their feet are light with dark tips.

INTERESTING FACTS

To call, this toad inflates a sac on its neck bigger than its head.

WHAT IT EATS

Great Plains toads eat slugs, spiders, moths, flies, beetles and grubs.

Take drinking water with you when you go exploring.

WOODHOUSE'S TOAD

They like swampy edges, slow rivers, ditches, reservoirs, cattle tanks and backyards.

They are more active at night than during the day. They hibernate by burrowing in loose soil and under plants and leaves.

Its sweet, short call sounds like the chuckling bleat of a sheep: "*Blaahh.....*"

WHAT IT LOOKS LIKE

This toad grows to be 2 to 4 inches long.

Its skin is olive-brown to greenish-gray. A whitish stripe runs down the center of the back. At least 1 large bump is in each dark spot on its back. The sides have dark spots, too.

Its head is thick and wide with a blunt nose. Its belly is tannish-yellow, usually without spots.

The tips of the toes are dark.

WHAT IT EATS

Woodhouse's toads are attracted to lights at night, where they find moths, worms, slugs and mosquitoes.

WHERE TO FIND IT

Woodhouse's toads live across the Great Plains south to Texas, Nevada and California. They are also found across the Southwest.

Wear boots, gloves and long pants.

OAK TOAD

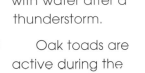

WHERE TO FIND IT

This toad likes scrubby pine areas from North Carolina to Florida, and west to Louisiana.

It is found under boards or logs, in small burrows, or near shallow pools that fill with water after a thunderstorm.

Oak toads are active during the day, especially after a heavy, warm rain.

These toads don't hibernate, so you may see them all year.

Oak toads have a chicken-like call that lasts about 10 seconds.

WHAT IT LOOKS LIKE

Oak toads are chunky. They grow from 3/4 to 1 1/4 inches long.

The bumpy skin is gray to blackish with golden spots. There is a yellow-white stripe down the back.

Pairs of tan to black spots run from the eyes down the back. The belly is creamy-gray.

The legs have black bands.

WHAT IT EATS

Oak toads like insects such as spiders, flies and ants.

INTERESTING FACTS

This is the smallest toad in North America.

Use the ruler on the back of this book to measure what you find.

FOWLER'S TOAD

WHAT IT LOOKS LIKE

The chubby Fowler's toad grows to be 2 to 3 inches long. It has a short, wide head.

The skin is gray-brown, greenish or brick red. There are dark spots with black edges. At least 3 bumps are in each large dark spot. There is also a light yellow stripe down the back.

The tan belly and chest usually have no spots.

It has long legs and long, slender toes.

WHERE TO FIND IT

Fowler's toads live along the Atlantic Coast from New Hampshire to North Carolina and west to Michigan. They are also found on the Gulf Coast from Louisiana to Oklahoma and north to Illinois.

They like warm, sandy edges around lakeshores, river valleys and ditches. They also like pastures, fields, gardens and sand dunes.

They come out after a warm, heavy rain and are active day and night. They hibernate in cold areas.

Its call is a dull buzz that can last up to 4 seconds. It sounds like "Waaahh."

WHAT IT EATS

Fowler's toads eat slugs, beetles, worms, flies, aphids and spiders.

Interesting Facts

Toads don't drink water very often. Most of it comes from the food they eat.

Wear a hat and use sunscreen to protect yourself from the sun.

SOUTHERN TOAD

WHERE TO FIND IT

Southern toads live from North Carolina to Florida, and west to Texas.

They like sandy fields and scrubby pine places. They are usually found near water, but not in it.

These toads do not hibernate. They are active more at dusk and at night than during the day.

The call is a high-pitched trill that lasts about 7 seconds.

WHAT IT LOOKS LIKE

This chunky toad grows to be 1 1/2 to 3 1/2 inches long.

The body is creamy-gray to reddish-black. The skin is rough and bumpy.

There are often dark streaks, blotches and stripes on its body. There is also a light stripe down the back. The belly is grayish.

It has slender feet and toes.

WHAT IT EATS

Southern toads like fireflies, locusts, spiders, crickets, grubs and small worms.

Watch for changes in weather.

MAKE A TOAD HOUSE

Toads like cool, moist places. You can make them a "house" that they will want to use during hot, dry weather.

WHAT YOU NEED

- A sheet of newspaper
- A chipped or cracked plastic flowerpot
- A pair of heavy scissors
- A permanent marker
- A fist-sized rock

WHAT TO DO

1 Spread the newspaper over your work area.

2 Using the marker, draw a doorway at the open edge of the flowerpot about the size of a silver dollar.

3 Using the scissors, cut carefully along the marked line. You may need an adult's help.

4 Take both the flowerpot and the rock outside. Put the flowerpot upside-down in a cool, shady area where it won't be bothered.

5 Pile loose dirt around the pot, but not across the doorway.

6 Put the rock on the flowerpot to help to hold it down all year long.

Your toad house is now ready for its special guest!

TURTLES

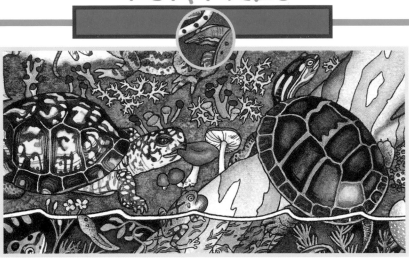

Turtles are reptiles. They move slowly on land compared to other animals. But they are swift and graceful in water.

Most turtles like freshwater lakes, ponds and rivers. They are also found on the land surrounding these and other wet places. Some turtles live in the ocean. Still others, called tortoises, prefer to stay on dry land all the time.

A turtle's favorite thing to do during the daytime is "bask." That means they like to rest and soak up warmth on top of a log or rock, or even each other!

The turtle's shell makes up as much as a third of the turtle's total weight. The shell is connected at the sides, with openings for the head, tail and legs.

Turtle shells are either bony or leathery. Some are rounded like an upside-down bowl. Others are almost flat. Whatever its shape, the shell protects the turtle's soft body.

To protect themselves from danger, some turtles can pull in their head and legs and hide inside their shells. Others can bite, hiss or scratch. So always be careful and don't get too close.

SNAPPING TURTLE

Snapping turtles often let other turtles bask on their backs.

WHERE TO FIND IT

Snappers live across the eastern, central and Gulf coastal United States, through Texas and west to Colorado, Wyoming and Montana.

They like shallow freshwater lakes, rivers and ponds. They also can be found along the soft bottoms and edges of deep water, such as reservoirs.

Snapping turtles are active day and night, floating on the water or creeping along the bottom. They hibernate in muddy lake and river bottoms.

WHAT IT LOOKS LIKE

This turtle can weigh 75 pounds and grow to be 2 feet long.

Its tan, olive-green or black shell has scallops along the rear edge. Young turtles have several rows of low, ridged bumps. Older turtles may have bumps that have been worn smooth. The turtle's underside is yellow-tan.

Its skin is tan to gray-black. The broad head is often covered with algae.

The thick legs have webbed toes, and claws. The long tail has thick saw-teeth on the edges.

WHAT IT EATS

Snapping turtles eat insects, crabs, fish, frogs, birds, snakes and plants.

DO NOT TOUCH.
This turtle bites hard and fast!

ALLIGATOR SNAPPING TURTLE

WHAT IT LOOKS LIKE

This turtle can grow to be 200 pounds and over 2 feet long, though most are much smaller.

The shell has rows of peaked ridges down its back. The shell is golden-brown to gray-green. The underside is yellow.

The skin is gray-black to tan. The head is large with a hooked beak.

The thick legs have webbed toes with claws. The long tail is thick.

WHERE TO FIND IT

Alligator snapping turtles live along the Gulf Coast from Georgia to Texas, and the Mississippi River valley north to Indiana and Illinois, west to Kansas.

They like the deep, quiet water of muddy rivers, lakes, canals and sloughs where they often lie on the bottom.

They are active day and night. They hibernate in cold climates inside muskrat lodges or under banks.

WHAT IT EATS

Alligator snappers eat fish, small alligators and water birds, clams, snakes, frogs and some plants.

INTERESTING FACTS

The alligator snapper "fishes" by opening its mouth underwater and wiggling a pink, worm-like piece of its tongue!

SPECIAL WARNING

DO NOT TOUCH. Snappers bite hard!

82

WESTERN PAINTED TURTLE

WHERE TO FIND IT

Western painted turtles live from Wisconsin and Illinois west across the Great Plains to Washington and Oregon.

They like slow-moving rivers and streams, with rocks or logs for basking.

They are active during early morning and late after-noon. They bask in groups at mid-day and sleep underwater at night. They hibernate under banks or in the muddy bottoms of pools and rivers.

WHAT IT LOOKS LIKE

Western painted turtles grow to be 4 to 9 inches long.

The shell is olive-green to black, with short, light bars around the edge. Yellow lines divide the smooth shell so that it looks like puzzle pieces.

The underside is reddish, with a dark blotch that spreads out at the edges.

The green skin has yellow and red streaks on the head and legs. The small head usually has a yellow spot behind each eye.

The clawed feet are webbed. The tail is short.

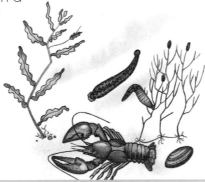

WHAT IT EATS

Western painted turtles eat water plants, leeches, crabs and clams.

Treat all animals with respect.

WOOD TURTLE

WHAT IT LOOKS LIKE

Wood turtles grow to be 8 inches long.

The rough shell looks like it is made up of little pyramids with black or yellow rings. The underside is yellow with brown blotches.

A wood turtle's skin is orange-red on top and tan-brown beneath. The black head is sleek and long.

The clawed feet are not webbed. The tail is medium-long.

WHAT IT EATS

Wood turtles eat worms, tadpoles, insects, berries and fungi.

WHERE TO FIND IT

Wood turtles live from New England to Virginia and across the upper Great Lakes west to Minnesota and Iowa.

They like moist woods and are often near water, not in it.

Wood turtles bask at midday on logs and sunny stream banks. They are active during early morning and late afternoon.

They hibernate in bottom mud or under logs in woods.

INTERESTING FACTS

Wood turtles are protected in some states.

Sometimes this turtle stamps its front feet on the ground and eats the earthworms that pop up.

Don't put your hand into any hole or burrow. It may be an animal's home.

SPINY SOFTSHELL TURTLE

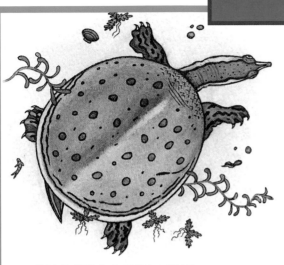

WHAT IT LOOKS LIKE

Spiny softshell turtles grow to be 20 inches long and can weigh up to 35 pounds.

The flat, olive-brown shell is hard, with softer edges. The shell looks like a pancake and feels like sandpaper. There are small, dark, spots on it and short spines on the front edge. The underside is usually light with a dark blotch.

The turtle's skin is olive to orange on top and gray-white underneath. It has a long neck. Its slender head has a tubelike snout. A yellow stripe runs up each side of the neck and through the eye.

The tail is short. The webbed feet have claws.

WHERE TO FIND IT

Spiny softshells live in the eastern, central and south-eastern United States, across the central Plains, west to Wyoming, Nevada and Texas. They are rare in the Northeast.

Softshells are active day and night, along shallow rivers and streams with swift currents.

They bask on sand banks and floating plants. In cold climates, they hibernate in bottom mud.

WHAT IT EATS

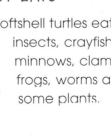

Softshell turtles eat insects, crayfish, minnows, clams, frogs, worms and some plants.

INTERESTING FACTS

Softshell turtles rest underwater, breathing through snouts that reach to the surface. They also breathe through their skin.

BOX TURTLE

WHAT IT LOOKS LIKE

Box turtles grow to be 4 to 7 inches long.

The olive-brown to dark brown shell is longer than it is wide. Eastern box turtle shells have orange or olive-green blotches. Others have yellow lines.

The underside is yellow with dark green streaks or smudges. The turtle's skin is gray-green to red-black with yellow or red-orange streaks. The head is chunky.

The tail is very short. The clawed feet are not webbed.

WHERE TO FIND IT

Eastern box turtles like open, moist woods south of the Great Lakes and the Mississippi River eastward to the Atlantic Coast. Other types of box turtles live in the plains and grasslands of the southwestern, central and south-central United States.

Box turtles live on land. They hide beneath damp, rotten logs during dry weather. They come out after a rain, sometimes to soak in mud. They are active during the day.

In cold areas, they hibernate in burrows, stumps or mud.

WHAT IT EATS

Box turtles eat worms, slugs, insects and snails. Some also eat the fruits, flowers, roots, seeds and leaves of plants.

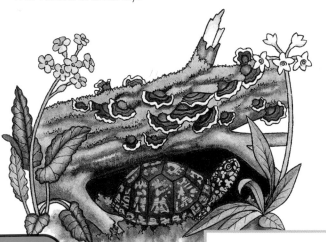

Don't leave behind any litter.

MAP TURTLE

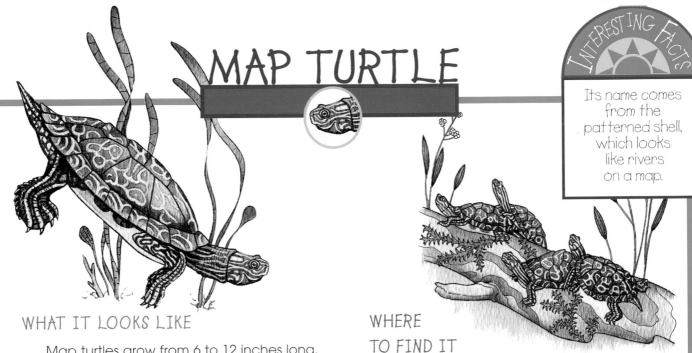

INTERESTING FACTS

Its name comes from the patterned shell, which looks like rivers on a map.

WHAT IT LOOKS LIKE

Map turtles grow from 6 to 12 inches long.

The mossy-green or brownish shell is flat and smooth with a ridge down the middle. It has thin yellow lines. The shell is jagged along the rear edge.

The skin is dark green with bright yellow stripes. Adult map turtles have a creamy yellow underside. Young turtles have a dark pattern underneath.

They have slender heads with a yellow spot behind each eye.

The tail is short. The feet are webbed and have claws.

WHERE TO FIND IT

Map turtles live in the Great Lakes region and along the Mississippi River. They are also found from the Ohio River valley to New England, south to Tennessee and Arkansas.

They like slow-moving rivers and lakes with floating logs and large rocks for sunning.

They are active in the morning and late afternoon. At midday, they gather to bask, often on top of one another. They hibernate in bottom mud.

WHAT IT EATS

Some types of map turtles eat only shellfish such as clams, crayfish and snails. Others eat insects, worms and some plants.

Watch out for poison ivy and poison oak.

87

BLANDING'S TURTLE

WHERE TO FIND IT

Blanding's turtles live in northern New England and west across the northern Great Lakes as far as Nebraska and South Dakota.

They like quiet streams and ponds, and marshes and sloughs with clean, firm bottoms. They bask on logs, muskrat houses, steep banks and driftwood.

Blanding's turtles are active during the day, especially in the morning. They sleep on pond bottoms or in floating plants at night. They hibernate in muskrat lodges and bottom mud.

WHAT IT LOOKS LIKE

Blanding's turtles grow to be 6 to 9 inches long.

The shiny, domed shell is dark black-green with many yellow speckles that can run together like streaks. The underside is yellow with green blotches along the edges.

The skin is green-gray. The head is sleek and small with a long neck. The jaw and neck are yellow underneath.

The webbed feet have claws. The tail is medium-long.

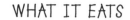

WHAT IT EATS

This turtle eats crayfish, frogs, insects, snails, worms and plants.

Be careful of turtles crossing the road.

RED-EARED TURTLE

WHAT IT LOOKS LIKE

Red-ears grow up to 9 inches long.

Its olive-brown shell is smooth and oval. It is splotched with red and yellow lines on its back. The rear edge of the shell is jagged. The yellowish underside has solid dark spots down its center.

The skin is olive-brown with orange-yellow stripes. Its small head has a red or yellow patch and stripe behind each eye.

The thick tail is medium-long. The webbed feet have claws.

WHERE TO FIND IT

Red-ears live from the mid-Atlantic states to the Gulf Coast and west into New Mexico. They are also found in the Mississippi River valley.

Red-ears like quiet, slow-moving rivers and ponds with muddy bottoms.

They are active in the morning and late afternoon. Red-ears rest at midday and at night. They bask on logs on top of one another.

Red-eared turtles hibernate in very cold weather, using muskrat lodges or underwater burrows. They come out to bask on warmer winter days.

WHAT IT EATS

Young red-ears eat insects, frogs, crayfish and worms. Adults prefer plants such as duckweed and other algae.

Use insect repellent to protect yourself.

EASTERN MUD TURTLE

WHERE TO FIND IT

Eastern mud turtles are found along the Atlantic Coast from New England to the Gulf Coast, and west to Louisiana. They also live in the Midwest from Illinois east to Pennsylvania. They are most common in parts of the southeastern states.

They like shallow, soft-bottomed bays, sloughs, canals, marshes and ponds, with lots of plants.

These turtles are active in the morning and evening. They do not bask much. Instead they crawl along the watery bottom or walk on land.

In northern areas, they hibernate in bottom mud, in burrows, or under plants.

WHAT IT LOOKS LIKE

Mud turtles grow up to 4 inches long.

The smooth, oval shell is yellow-brown to black. It looks like it's divided into pieces of a jigsaw puzzle. The underside is orange to yellow-brown and usually has a black center with dark blotches.

The skin is olive-brown and blotchy. It has a chunky head.

All four feet are webbed and have claws. The mud turtle has a short, thick tail.

WHAT IT EATS

Mud turtles eat water insect larvae, crabs, clams and fish. Some also eat algae and water plants.

INTERESTING FACTS

Mud turtles smell like wet earth.

Use the Scrapbook to draw what you see.

GOPHER TORTOISE

WHAT IT LOOKS LIKE

Gopher tortoises grow to be about 1 foot long.

The shell is a smooth dome. It is brown or black with rings. The underside is yellowish.

It has a horny spur on the front under the neck. The skin is orange to gray-brown.

The head is large and rounded.

The chubby legs are scaly. The toes are not webbed. They have claws. The tail is short and fat.

WHERE TO FIND IT

Gopher tortoises live in open, dry, sandy woods along the Gulf Coast from South Carolina to Louisiana. They also like scrubby beach areas.

They are out during late-morning, rainy or not. The rest of its time is spent in the burrow.

They are active all year and do not hibernate.

WHAT IT EATS

The gopher tortoise eats grasses, berries, fruits, seeds and leaves.

Tell an adult where you are going and how long you will be gone.

DESERT TORTOISE

WHERE TO FIND IT

Desert tortoises live in the canyons and dry rocky hillsides of Nevada, California, Utah and Arizona.

They are active at midday and late afternoon and after a summer rainstorm.

They spend much time in their burrows. In cold weather, desert tortoises hibernate in group burrows.

WHAT IT LOOKS LIKE

Desert tortoises grow to be about 12 inches long.

The domed shell is black to tan. It may have brown or orange marks. The underside is black to tan with some yellowish blotches and dark lines.

The neck skin is yellowish, the large, round head is tan to red.

There is a horny spur sticking out from the front of its underside.

The brown legs are chubby. The toes have claws. The tail is short and thick.

INTERESTING FACTS

Desert tortoises are endangered in some states.

Desert tortoises can live a whole year without drinking any water.

WHAT IT EATS

Desert tortoises eat desert flowers, cacti, grasses and berries.

Take this book and a pencil along when you go exploring.

GREEN TURTLE

WHERE TO FIND IT

Green turtles live in the Atlantic Ocean from Maine to the Florida Keys. They are also found from Alaska southward in the Pacific Ocean. They feed near shallow river mouths like San Diego Bay and around island groups, such as Hawaii.

They are active in these shallows in morning and late afternoon. Green turtles do not hibernate.

WHAT IT LOOKS LIKE

Green turtles can grow to be 4 feet long and weigh almost 900 pounds!

The olive-brown to black shell often has brown blotches. The underside is white or yellowish.

The skin is brown to gray-black. Its head is small.

The legs look like flippers. There is one claw on each foot. The tail is short and thick.

WHAT IT EATS

Green turtles eat turtle grass and other sea plants, algae and red mangrove roots and leaves.

INTERESTING FACTS

Green turtles are endangered.

The green turtle travels more than 1,000 miles between its feeding and resting places.

Don't disturb turtle nests or hatchlings.

MAKE A TURTLE PAPERWEIGHT

You can keep a "turtle" in your house by making this fun paperweight. Try using different sizes of paper plates for little turtles and big turtles.

WHAT YOU NEED

- A sheet of newspaper

- Two matching paper plates with smooth, flat edges (not rippled)

- A cup of clean, dry pebbles

- A bottle of white glue

- Crayons

- Scraps of green or brown felt

- Scissors

WHAT TO DO

1 Spread the newspaper over your work area.

2 Using the crayons, color the bottom of one paper plate in your favorite turtle's shell colors.

3 Color the bottom of the other paper plate to be your turtle's underside.

4 Lay the paper plate for the top shell colored-side down.

5 Pour the pebbles into the middle of it.

6 Spread a thick layer of glue along the edge of the paper plate.

7 Lay the other paper plate, colored-side up, over it so the flat edges touch. Press the two edges to seal. Let dry.

8 Use the scissors to cut the felt scraps into shapes for the head, neck, tail and feet.

9 Glue them in place on the bottom of your turtle. Let dry.

Turn your turtle over.
It is now ready to sit in a special place.

SCRAPBOOK

Frogs, Toads and Turtles

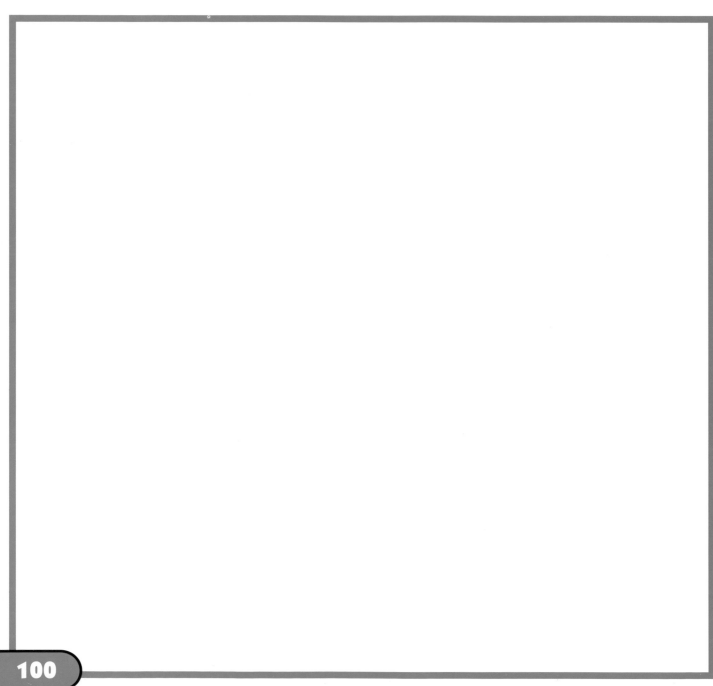

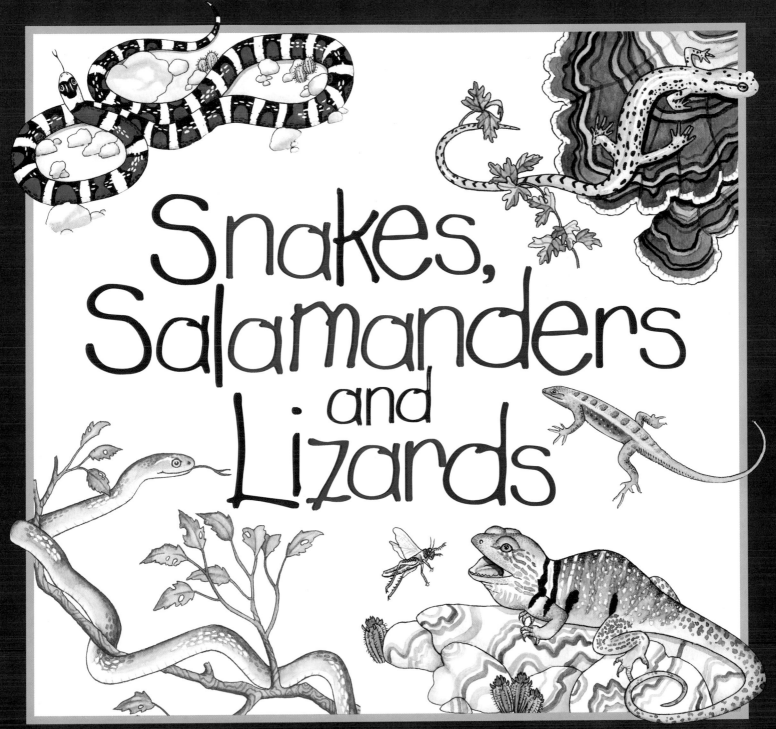

Snakes, Salamanders and Lizards

by Diane L. Burns

illustrations by Linda Garrow

SNAKES

Snakes are animals known as reptiles. Reptiles have skin made up of scales.

They are cold-blooded. The air temperature decides their body temperature. If the air is too cold or too warm, the snake will die.

Snakes have scales that are clean and dry. The skin does not stretch as the snake grows. The snake must shed its skin at least once a year.

Snakes hibernate in cold weather. They have no arms or legs. Snakes use small, hooked teeth to grab and hold their food.

Each side of a snake's lower jaw moves. This lets the snake eat food bigger than its mouth.

Snakes sense odors with their tongues.

There are about 115 different kinds of snakes in the United States.

Most snakes are harmless. Some are poisonous.

Most snakes squeeze their prey to death and swallow it whole. Poisonous snakes use their venom to kill prey.

Tell an adult where you are going or take one with you.

COMMON GARTER SNAKE

Tips to find this snake

Garter snakes are usually found in fields or grassy woods.

On warm days, they rest in sunny spots.

Garter snakes are active during the day.

WHAT IT LOOKS LIKE

In the East, garter snakes have yellow stripes on their dark bodies. In the West, both the stripes and their bodies may be red-orange. Sometimes, their heads are red. The stripes on all garter snakes run the length of their bodies.

They grow to be 4 feet long. Garter snakes are pencil-thin and look fragile.

WHAT IT EATS

Garter snakes eat earthworms, slugs, birds, grasshoppers, and small rodents like mice.

WHERE IT LIVES

Garter snakes are found everywhere in the United States except for the southwestern deserts.

INTERESTING FACTS

The garter snake is named for old-fashioned garters, which men once used to hold up their socks.

SPECIAL WARNING

They will bite if threatened. Be careful!

GREEN SNAKE

Tips to find this snake

Green snakes are active during the day.

On warm days, they may be found in meadows and pastures.

They also live close to the ground near ponds and streams.

WHAT IT LOOKS LIKE

These snakes are hard to see. Whether lying still or zipping away, they blend in. Their bodies are bright green on top. They are pale yellow-white on their bellies.

Green snakes are slender, and about 2 feet long.

WHAT IT EATS

Green snakes eat spiders, caterpillars, and grasshoppers.

WHERE IT LIVES

Green snakes are found in the northeastern and central United States and south to Florida and the Gulf Coast into Texas.

Get permission before going onto someone's land.

WATER SNAKE

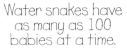

Water snakes have as many as 100 babies at a time.

Tips to find this snake

During warm spring and summer days, water snakes rest in the sun.

Look for water snakes on logs, or on branches hanging over water.

Water snakes like ditches, canals, marshes, ponds, bayous, and lakes.

WHAT IT LOOKS LIKE

Their bodies are usually solid brown on top, but they can also be grayish or blue-black. Some have light and dark brown diamond shapes on them.

Sometimes, there are dark brown crossbands on its body or belly. The water snake's belly is likely to be either red or yellow.

They are thin snakes that grow to be 2 to 3 feet long.

WHAT IT EATS

Water snakes eat small fish and frogs.

WHERE IT LIVES

Water snakes are found in the Mississippi River valley and the Great Lakes region. They also live in the south-eastern United States west into Texas, Oklahoma, and Kansas.

SPECIAL WARNING

Don't touch! They will bite. Wear boots!

KINGSNAKE

Tips to find this snake

Kingsnakes are most active in early morning or early evening, especially in hot weather.

Sometimes they hide under rocks.

The harmless eastern milk snake (which is a kind of kingsnake) looks like the poisonous copperhead.

Kingsnakes often look like the deadly coral snake. Here is a good rhyme to remember how to tell them apart:

"Red touch yellow, kill a fellow. Red touch black, venom lack."

That means if a red stripe is touching a yellow stripe, the snake is a dangerous coral snake. And you should stay away.

WHAT IT LOOKS LIKE

Kingsnakes can be black, brown, or red. They have blotches or bands or speckles.

Kingsnakes have thick bodies and grow from 3 to 6 feet long.

WHAT IT EATS

Kingsnakes find birds, lizards, and rodents to be tasty treats.

WHERE IT LIVES

Kingsnakes are found throughout the United States, in swamps, forests, plains, deserts, and mountains.

Special Warning

Don't touch or approach!

RATTLESNAKE

Tips to find this snake

Rattlesnakes are active at night.

During the day, they rest in the shade of rocks and logs.

You can see them only from May through September. They hibernate during the other months.

WHAT IT LOOKS LIKE

The body of a rattler is brown-gray, and it is thick and solid. Dark blotches or diamond shapes along the back and sides of its body are usually edged in dark brown.

The rattlesnake grows from 4 to 8 feet long.

WHAT IT EATS

Rattlers eat small rodents such as mice, and birds that like to stay close to the ground.

WHERE IT LIVES

Some types of rattlesnakes live east of the Mississippi River. They like forests and rocky highlands. Some also live in swampy areas.

Rattlesnakes west of the Mississippi live in the deserts and mountains. They also like dry, rocky buttes.

SPECIAL WARNING

A rattlesnake bite is poisonous. If you hear its tail rattling, stay away!

COPPERHEAD

WHAT IT LOOKS LIKE

Copperheads have thick bodies the color of toasted marshmallows. On its back and sides are red-brown hourglass-shaped blotches.

Copperheads grow to be 2 to 3 feet long.

WHAT IT EATS

Copperheads eat mice, rabbits, lizards, and frogs.

WHERE IT LIVES

Copperheads are found from Massachusetts south to Georgia, and west as far as Kansas and Texas.

Tips to find this snake

Copperheads are usually active during the day. But, during very hot weather they are active at night.

In spring and fall, copperheads are found around rocks and in dry, deep woods.

In summer, copperheads like cool and wet areas.

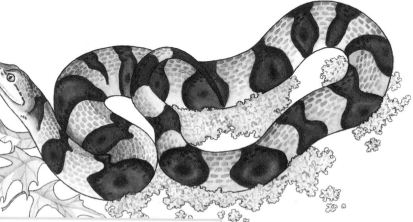

SPECIAL WARNING

The copperhead's bite is poisonous!
Do not approach!

HOGNOSE SNAKE

Tips to find this snake

Hognose snakes like dry sandy places, like open woods and fields or sandpits.

Look for them in areas that have dead leaves on the ground, too.

SPECIAL NOTE

A hognose may try to scare you by hissing and puffing out its head. Don't tease it.

WHAT IT LOOKS LIKE

Sometimes their body color is solid. It can be gray, green, rusty red, or brown. Hognoses sometimes have blotchy patterns on their backs in gray, brown, or black. The belly color is usually lighter than the body color.

They have thick bodies and grow to be 2 to 4 feet long.

WHAT IT EATS

Hognoses eat toads, mice, and birds.

WHERE IT LIVES

Hognose snakes are found everywhere in the United States except in the western mountains and deserts.

SPECIAL WARNING

Sometimes, they bite. Don't touch! Their saliva is not poisonous, but it can be harmful.

BULLSNAKE

This snake gets its name from its hiss, which sounds like a grunting bull.

Bullsnakes eat rats and mice in barns and sheds, so farmers and ranchers like them.

Tips to find this snake

Bullsnakes are active during the day.

Besides farmland, they like sandy pine woods and prairies.

WHAT IT LOOKS LIKE

Its yellow-tan body has large, red-brown blotches along the back and sides.

Bullsnakes have heavy, solid bodies and grow to be about 10 feet long.

WHAT IT EATS

Bullsnakes eat small rodents, birds, and young rabbits.

WHERE IT LIVES

Bullsnakes are found on the Great Plains.

A kind of bullsnake known as the gopher snake is found in the western United States.

A type of bullsnake known as the pine snake is found in the eastern United States.

SPECIAL WARNING

Bullsnakes will strike if bothered. Don't get too close!

110

CORN SNAKE

Tips to find this snake

The corn snake is active at night.

It likes barns and ditches where it can find food and shelter.

It hides during the day in gopher burrows or under logs or rocks.

WHAT IT LOOKS LIKE

The corn snake's body is yellow-brown to gray. It has red-brown saddle-shaped blotches along its back and sides. Its belly has black bars or checker-shapes on it.

Its sturdy and solid body can grow to be 2 to 4 feet long.

WHAT IT EATS

Corn snakes eat small animals such as mice, birds, and rabbits.

WHERE IT LIVES

Corn snakes can be found from New Jersey south to Florida, west to Nebraska and New Mexico.

INTERESTING FACTS

This snake got its name by often being found in corn fields.

Don't approach or touch any wild animals you might see.

RAT SNAKE

Tips to find this snake

Rat snakes like woods, rocky hillsides and farmyards.

In spring and fall, the snake is active during the day.

In summer it is active at night.

It may be found in barns and stables where it looks for mice and rats to eat.

INTERESTING FACTS

Rat snakes have this name because they eat many rodents.

They like to climb, so look up—in rafters and beams, and in trees.

WHAT IT LOOKS LIKE

Some rat snakes have solid black bodies. Some have red, yellow or gray bodies with 4 dark stripes from head to tail. Others have a tannish body with dark blotches. All rat snakes have tan bellies.

Rat snakes have thick, sturdy bodies and grow to be 3 to 6 feet long.

WHAT IT EATS

Rat snakes eat frogs, mice, small rabbits, and lizards.

WHERE IT LIVES

They are found from Maine south along the east coast into Florida, also west to Texas and north to Iowa.

SPECIAL WARNING

They bite if threatened.

MAKE A DRIED BEAN PICTURE

WHAT YOU NEED

- piece of posterboard about 12 x 18 inches large

- fine-point marker

- bottle of glue

- dried beans and peas: kidney beans are red, black beans are black, split peas are green, navy beans are white, lentils are yellow, and pinto beans spotted.

- newspaper

- damp washcloth

- masking tape for hanging

WHAT TO DO

1 Spread the newspaper over your workspace.

2 Divide up the beans and peas, putting each color in a pile.

3 Use this book to choose a snake, a salamander, or a lizard.

4 With the marker, draw the outline of the animal onto the posterboard.

5 Draw its bands or blotches or spots of color.

6 Spread glue on one of the spots or blotches, using your fingers.

7 Wipe your fingers clean with the damp washcloth.

8 Carefully place the beans with colors matching the picture onto the glue.

9 Make sure to put the beans close together.

10 Repeat with the other sections, making sure to use the right colors.

11 Let the finished picture dry, then hang it on your wall or door.

SALAMANDERS

Salamanders are animals known as amphibians. Amphibians have smooth skin. They can live on land and in the water.

About 135 kinds of salamanders live in the United States.

They have long tails and long bodies.

Most salamanders have 4 legs. Others have only 2 legs. Some have no legs.

Most are active at night.

They have 4 toes on each front foot.

Most salamanders have 5 toes on each hind foot. The toes do not have claws.

All salamanders avoid the sun.

They can repair almost any injury to their bodies.

They can regrow new tails, legs, and feet.

Be kind to all animals.

MUDPUPPY

Tips to find this salamander

Mudpuppies live only in cool, fresh water like streams.

At night, look in the streambed while they are feeding.

During the day, they hide under rocks in the stream.

Mudpuppies are active all year, even in winter.

WHAT IT LOOKS LIKE

A mudpuppy has a grayish to dark brown smooth body. It has 3 red, frilly gills on each side of the head.

Mudpuppies can grow to be 15 inches long. They have 4 short legs.

WHAT IT EATS

Mudpuppies eat crayfish, insects, worms, and fish.

WHERE IT LIVES

Mudpuppies live throughout the north-eastern United States, and through the Great Lakes down to Kansas and southern Missouri.

Use the ruler on the back of this book to measure what you find.

SIREN

Tips to find this salamander

Sirens live in warm, still water such as ditches and swamps.

Sirens are most active at night.

They hide during the day under rocks and logs, and among water plants.

WHAT IT LOOKS LIKE

The siren's slender dark gray-brown body has black spots. It has 3 pairs of blue-gray gills just behind the head.

A siren looks like an eel. Its body grows from 6 inches long to as much as 50 inches. It has 2 tiny front feet, but no back feet.

WHAT IT EATS

Sirens eat crayfish, worms, clams, and some water plants.

WHERE IT LIVES

Sirens are found along the coastal southeastern United States from South Carolina and Florida, west to Texas and up the Mississippi River valley.

Pay attention to everything around you.

TIGER SALAMANDER

Tips to find this salamander

Tiger salamanders live in grassy or swampy burrows.

In spring, they travel at night to shallow ponds.

During rainy times, look for them under rocks or logs. They may even lie in window wells or wander across roads.

INTERESTING FACTS

Tiger salamanders are the largest land salamanders in the world.

Some young tiger salamanders eat each other! Maybe it is their big appetite that gives them their name.

WHAT IT LOOKS LIKE

The tiger salamander has smooth, dark-brown or black skin. It has white, gold, or greenish spots and blotches on top. Underneath, its belly is green-yellow. The body is thick, and the head is wide.

A tiger salamander grows to be 13 inches long. It has 4 short, stout legs.

WHAT IT EATS

Tiger salamanders always seem to be hungry.

They like worms, mice, and insects such as crickets.

WHERE IT LIVES

Tiger salamanders are found across the United States, but they are rare in the Appalachian mountains, the north-eastern and Pacific states.

Wear boots, gloves and long pants.

SPOTTED SALAMANDER

Tips to find this salamander

Spotted salamanders like quiet forests with ponds.

Spotted salamanders are active at night, especially along pond edges in late winter.

WHAT IT LOOKS LIKE

The spotted salamander has a black or dark brown body. It has an uneven row of yellow or orange spots along each side of its body (but none on the belly). The belly is gray-blue and lightly speckled. Its body is thick, with shallow dents along its body.

Spotted salamanders are usually 6 to 10 inches long. They have 4 chubby legs.

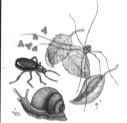

WHAT IT EATS

Spotted salamanders eat insects, earth worms, snails, and spiders.

WHERE IT LIVES

Spotted salamanders live in the eastern United States as far west as the Texas/Oklahoma border, and north to the Great Lakes region.

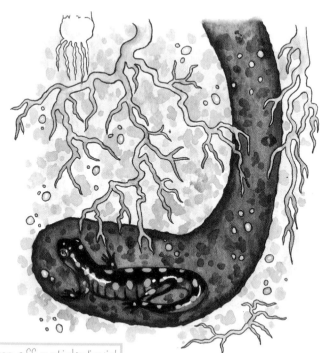

SPECIAL WARNING

Do not handle! Its skin gives off a sticky liquid that is bad-tasting and harmful to other animals.

118

RED EFT

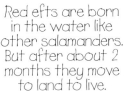

Tips to find this salamander

Red efts are easiest to find in September and October, just before the winter frost. At this time, young red efts leave the ponds for their years on land. Look under rocks and logs in woods for them.

Also In September and October, mature red efts head to freshwater ponds. Their skin color changes from red-orange to green-brown.

INTERESTING FACTS

Red efts are born in the water like other salamanders. But after about 2 months they move to land to live.

After 2 to 3 years the adult is now called a red-spotted newt. It then moves back into the water to live.

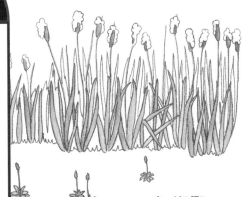

WHAT IT LOOKS LIKE

Red efts have red-orange bodies. There are a few small red spots on its back and sides. Its skin is rough and dry, not slimy.

The red eft grows to be 1-1/2 inches to 3-1/2 inches long, and is slender in shape with a worm-like tail. It has 4 short, slender legs.

WHAT IT EATS

Red efts eat small worms, and insects such as flies.

WHERE IT LIVES

Red efts are found east of the Mississippi River.

SPECIAL WARNING

Do not touch! Your mouth and eyes will sting and burn if you touch them after touching a red eft.

FOUR-TOED SALAMANDER

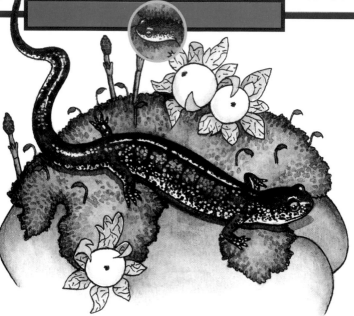

Its name comes from having only 4 toes on each hind foot. (Most salamanders have 5.)

When it is threatened, the four-toed salamander waves its tail in the air to scare the enemy.

Tips to find this salamander

Four-toed salamanders are active at night.

They like wet and muddy ground where moss covers rotting logs.

Four-toed salamanders hide in moss in late summer.

WHAT IT LOOKS LIKE

The four-toed salamander has red-brown skin that looks speckled along its gray sides. Its white belly looks as if it is sprinkled with pepper.

The body is slender and grows to be 2-1/2 to 4 inches long. Four-toed salamanders have 4 short, slender legs.

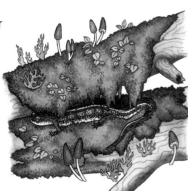

WHAT IT EATS

It eats small spiders, insects, and worms.

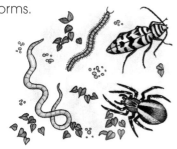

WHERE IT LIVES

Four-toed salamanders live east of the Mississippi River.

Wear boots! Take a flashlight. Carefully peel back the moss while you are searching. Always put back any moss you disturb.

TWO-LINED SALAMANDER

Tips to find this salamander

Look along the edges of small streams and creeks.

It is active at night when it looks for food.

Sometimes, it climbs short plants to find food.

WHAT IT EATS

Two-lined salamanders eat small water insects and snails.

WHERE IT LIVES

Two-lined salamanders live in the Appalachian Mountains of the southeastern United States.

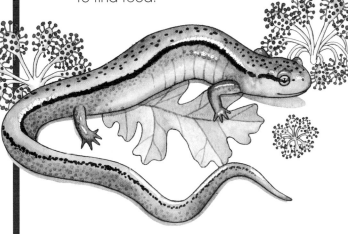

WHAT IT LOOKS LIKE

The two-lined salamander is tan, with black stripes on the top of each side. It has a slender and narrow body.

It grows to be 2 to 4 inches long. It has a long tail and 4 short, skinny legs.

Take this book and a pencil when you go exploring.

SLIMY SALAMANDER

Tips to find this salamander

Slimy salamanders like cool, moist areas such as rocky banks or caves.

They can also be found under flat rocks or logs.

They come out at night to feed.

They are especially active in wet weather.

WHAT IT LOOKS LIKE

Slimy salamanders have blue-black skin with white speckles. They have thin, smooth bodies.

They grow to be about 7 inches long with 4 short, skinny legs.

WHAT IT EATS

Slimy salamanders eat ants, beetles, earthworms, and slugs.

WHERE IT LIVES

Slimy salamanders live from New England south to the Gulf Coast, southwest to Oklahoma, and into central Texas.

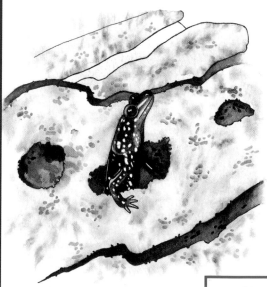

Always bring drinking water with you.

LONGTAIL SALAMANDER

Tips to find this salamander

They like moist, sheltered places like cracks between rocks.

Look in rocky banks, and under rocks near ponds and streams too.

They hide during the day and come out in early evening to eat.

Sometimes, they climb logs and tree-trunks looking for food.

WHAT IT LOOKS LIKE

The longtail salamander's skin is yellow-orange with dark brown or black spots. The spots form V's on the long tail. Its belly is yellow and usually not spotted.

Longtail salamanders can grow to be 6 inches long. They have thin bodies with 4 short, skinny legs.

WHAT IT EATS

They eat small insects such as spiders and worms.

WHERE IT LIVES

Longtail salamanders live from southern New York state to northern Alabama, and from the Atlantic coast west to Missouri.

INTERESTING FACTS

The longtail salamander gets its name from its very long tail.

SPECIAL NOTE
Take a flashlight! The light will not bother this salamander, so you can watch it. Wear boots—you might be in wet places.

Watch where you step.

MARBLED SALAMANDER

Tips to find this salamander

Look in dry woods beneath
leaf piles and logs,
and in burrows.

During summer and autumn,
marbled salamanders
guard the eggs they have
laid in dried-up ponds.

WHAT IT LOOKS LIKE

Marbled salamanders have dark brown to
black bellies. Their bodies are white along
the top, with chocolate brown blotches.

Its body is pudgy and grows to be about 5
inches long. It has 4 thick, short legs.

INTERESTING FACTS

Marbled
salamander adults
can't swim but
their babies
live in water.

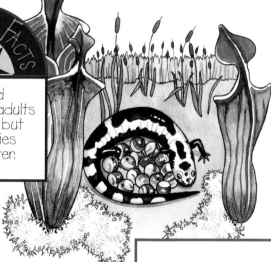

WHAT IT EATS

Marbled salamanders eat
grubs and insects
such as spiders.

WHERE IT LIVES

Marbled salamanders live
from Florida west to Texas
along the Gulf Coast,
and north to the Great Lakes
and the New England states.

Don't leave behind any litter.

MAKE A "STAINED GLASS" ANIMAL

WHAT YOU NEED

- newspaper

- bottle of glue

- black construction paper

- scissors

- tissue paper in different colors

- masking tape for hanging

- white crayon

WHAT TO DO

1 Spread the newspaper over your work area.

2 Use this book to choose a salamander, a snake, or a lizard with bright spots or blotches.

3 Draw the outline of the animal you choose onto the black construction paper, using the white crayon. Also draw its spots or blotches. You can make the animal larger on the paper than it really is.

4 Using the scissors, cut along the outline.

5 Then, cut out each of the spots and blotches with the scissors, so the animal outline looks "holey."

6 Next, cut out bigger shapes from the colored tissue paper.

7 Put glue around the edge of each hole and stick a piece of tissue in place on the back side of the outline.

8 Let the glue dry.

9 Using the masking tape, tape your "stained glass" animal to a window where the light can shine through the tissue paper.

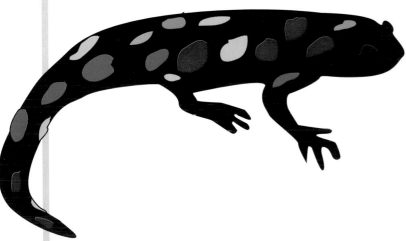

LIZARDS

Lizards, like snakes, are animals known as reptiles.

There are about 90 kinds of lizards in the United States.

Lizards have long bodies and long tails.

They usually have 4 legs. Others have 2 legs. Some lizards have no legs.

Usually, lizards have 5 toes on each front foot.

The toes have claws.

Lizard skin is dry. It is covered with scales.

Some lizards are very fast, and can run up to 15 miles per hour!

Most can also swim.

If their tail is broken off, they can grow a new one.

Don't hurry. Take your time and have fun!

SKINK

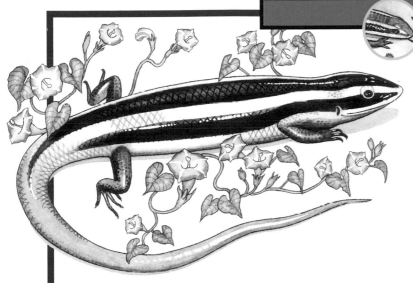

Tips to find this lizard

Skinks like undisturbed places, such as rock piles and vacant lots.

Look for them from spring through fall only. They hibernate in the winter.

They are active during the day, especially when it is warm.

WHAT IT LOOKS LIKE

Some skinks have a solid body color. Others have lines that run the length of the body. Smooth, flat scales give its body a glossy shine.

Skinks grow to be about 12 inches long. Some look like a snake or worm with very short legs.

WHAT IT EATS

Most skinks eat grubs and insects such as ants and worms.

Some skinks also eat plants.

WHERE IT LIVES

Skinks can be found all over the United States, except for the high western mountains.

INTERESTING FACTS

Skinks have scales with little pieces of bone in them, so all together they are like a suit of armor.

Some skinks have no legs and burrow underground.

Tell an adult how long you will be gone.

FENCE LIZARD

Tips to find this lizard

Fence lizards like quiet places like rock piles and fences around pastures.

They also live in trees and shrubs.

They are active during the day.

WHAT IT LOOKS LIKE

Fence lizards are gray or brown. Some have uneven black V's on their back and tail. Males have at least 1 blue patch on the throat.

Fence lizards grow to be 3 to 8 inches long. They have slender bodies and long tails.

WHAT IT EATS

Fence lizards eat insects such as spiders.

WHERE IT LIVES

Fence lizards live from Delaware south to Florida and west to Arizona.

INTERESTING FACTS

Fence lizards are nicknamed "swifts" because they are hard to catch.

Lift rocks away from you when exploring.

BANDED GECKO

Tips to find this lizard

Banded geckos are active at night from June through September. They hibernate during other months.

They like rocky, sand deserts.

They hide during the day under rocks, boards, or litter.

WHAT IT LOOKS LIKE

A banded gecko has a cream-colored body with brown blotches across its back and sides. The skin is soft. Its body is covered with fine scales that look like beads.

Banded geckos grow to be about 6 inches long. They have thin bodies with long tails.

WHAT IT EATS

Banded geckos eat small insects such as spiders.

WHERE IT LIVES

Geckos live in the southwestern deserts and canyons, from California east to Texas.

Don't approach or touch any wild plants you don't know. Stay away from poison ivy and poison oak.

GREEN ANOLE

Tips to find this lizard

It is active during the day.

Anoles climb trees, shrubs, fences, and also walls of old buildings.

They like shady places when it is hot.

SPECIAL NOTE
Look for this animal during or after a rain. The green anole gets all of its water from droplets it licks off places like leaves or posts.

WHAT IT LOOKS LIKE

Green anoles vary in color from bright green to dark brown. Males have a pink flap of skin on the throat.

The anole grows to be about 5 to 8 inches long and has a thin body. Its head has a narrow snout.

WHAT IT EATS

Anoles eat insects such as cockroaches, crickets, and flies.

WHERE IT LIVES

Anoles live from southern Virginia south to Florida, and west to Texas and Oklahoma.

SPECIAL WARNING
Anoles like to jump— don't be surprised when they do!

COLLARED LIZARD

Tips to find this lizard

Collared lizards are active during the day.

They like dry rock piles and gullies.

Look for them on sunny days, resting on rocks.

WHAT IT LOOKS LIKE

The collared lizard has a lime green body with brown stripes across its back. Collared lizards have large heads.

It grows to be about 12 inches long with a heavy, solid body and a long skinny tail.

WHAT IT EATS

Collared lizards eat small lizards and large insects like grasshoppers.

WHERE IT LIVES

Collared lizards live west of the Mississippi River and less commonly in the southeastern states.

INTERESTING FACTS

This lizard is named for the 2 black rings that look like a collar around its neck.

The collared lizard stands up and runs on its back legs.

SPECIAL WARNING

They will bite if you try to touch them. Be careful!

SIDE-BLOTCHED LIZARD

Tips to find this lizard

Side-blotched lizards like rocky places.

They use packrat burrows to escape the desert midday heat.

They are active in cool morning hours and in the late afternoon.

In the spring, males perch on large rocks and watch for other males that might trespass in their territory.

WHAT IT LOOKS LIKE

The side blotched lizard's skin is tannish-brown with light-colored spots. The slender body is covered with fine, overlapping scales.

Side-blotched lizards grow to be about 6 inches long.

WHAT IT EATS

Side-blotched lizards eat small insects such as black ants, beetles, locusts, and flies.

They even eat scorpions!

WHERE IT LIVES

Side-blotched lizards are found from California and Arizona into Utah and north-west to Washington. They also live in New Mexico and Texas.

INTERESTING FACTS

Their name comes from the blotch of blue or black behind each front leg.

Don't put your hand into any holes or burrows or cracks. They may be animals' homes.

LEOPARD LIZARD

Tips to find this lizard

Leopard lizards like dry, open, flat ground.

On hot days, look for them in the shade of a plant.

WHAT IT LOOKS LIKE

Leopard lizards have black blotches and small red patches over a brown body. Their bellies are light brown or gray.

They grow to be about 8 to 15 inches long and are slender.

INTERESTING FACTS

The leopard lizard gets its name from the many spots on its body.

WHAT IT EATS

Leopard lizards eat large insects such as grasshoppers, and smaller lizards (even other leopard lizards).

They also eat berries.

WHERE IT LIVES

Leopard lizards live in the desert areas of southern Oregon and Idaho, south into California and southeast to Texas.

Do not touch—they will bite!

SPECIAL WARNING

HORNED LIZARD

Tips to find this lizard

It is active only during the day.

Horned lizards are hard to see. Their blotchy skin helps them blend in.

Look on rocks, where they wait for prey to pass by.

Sometimes, they lie half-buried in the sand or under a cactus.

They like flat, sandy, open areas.

SPECIAL NOTE

If startled, the horned lizard may run a short ways and then freeze, blending in again.

When threatened, it may spray blood from the corners of its eyes at its enemy.

INTERESTING FACTS

The horned lizard uses its sticky tongue to pick up poisonous ants without harming itself.

It gets its name from the "horns" across the top of its head.

It looks like a small dinosaur!

WHAT IT LOOKS LIKE

The blotchy, brown and tan skin has spines on the head and also along the sides of the body. The body is rounded with a short tail. Their muscular legs and clawed feet are used for digging.

Horned lizards grow to be about 4 inches long.

WHAT IT EATS

Ants, crickets, sow bugs, and other small insects are food for the horned lizard.

WHERE IT LIVES

Horned lizards live in desert areas of the western and southwestern United States (including Texas) and north to Kansas.

SPECIAL WARNING

Be careful of the sharp spines! Don't touch!

GILA MONSTER

WHAT IT LOOKS LIKE

The gila monster has a dark brown body with pale orange blotches. The belly is black. Their skin looks beaded. Its body is broad, and it has a long tail.

The gila monster is big! It grows to be 1 to 2 feet long.

WHAT IT EATS

Gila monsters eat small birds, mice, insects, and eggs. It also eats dead animals.

WHERE IT LIVES

Gila monsters live in Nevada, Arizona, California, Utah, Texas, and New Mexico.

Tips to find this lizard

Gila monsters like rocky deserts, canyons near water, and scrubby forests.

Sometimes they climb trees looking for food.

Gila monsters are most active at dawn or dusk.

They hide under large rocks during the heat of the day.

Don't touch! Don't get too close.

Venom is released as the Gila monster bites and chews. The bite can be fatal to dogs and harmful to you.

Gila monsters have a strong grip. If it is provoked it will grab on and not let go!

SPECIAL WARNING

INTERESTING FACTS

The gila monster is the only lizard in the United States that is poisonous.

The gila monster smells with its tongue!

Gila monsters sleep on their backs with their legs sprawled out.

CHUCKWALLA

Tips to find this lizard

Chuckwallas live in large rock slabs, like blocks of lava, where there are many cracks.

They are active during the day.

WHAT IT LOOKS LIKE

The chuckwalla's yellowish skin looks mud-splattered. It has loose skin along the neck and body. It has a flat body with a long skinny tail.

The chuckwalla is a big lizard. It can grow to be 1 to 2 feet long.

WHAT IT EATS

Chuckwallas eat the buds, flowers and leaves of plants.

WHERE IT LIVES

Chuckwallas live in southern California, north into Nevada, Utah, and Arizona.

Wear a hat and use sunscreen to protect yourself from the sun.

MAKE A CLAY MODEL

WHAT YOU NEED

- a flat surface, such as a table, that will not be damaged by clay

- popsicle stick

- fork

- stick of modeling clay

- plastic bag

- damp washcloth

WHAT TO DO

1 On the flat surface, shape the clay into your favorite animals from this book. Snakes can be made by rolling clay into a long rope.

2 Use the popsicle stick and the fork to add details to the animal's "skin," like a scaly pattern, lines, or bumps. The fork can be used to add eyes and toes.

3 The animals can be shown sleeping or hunting. You can change the shape or the position many times.

4 When you are finished playing, store the clay in the plastic bag.

5 Clean up the surface and your hands with the washcloth.

6 If you have the kind of clay that gets hard, you can let your animal dry and keep it forever.

SCRAPBOOK

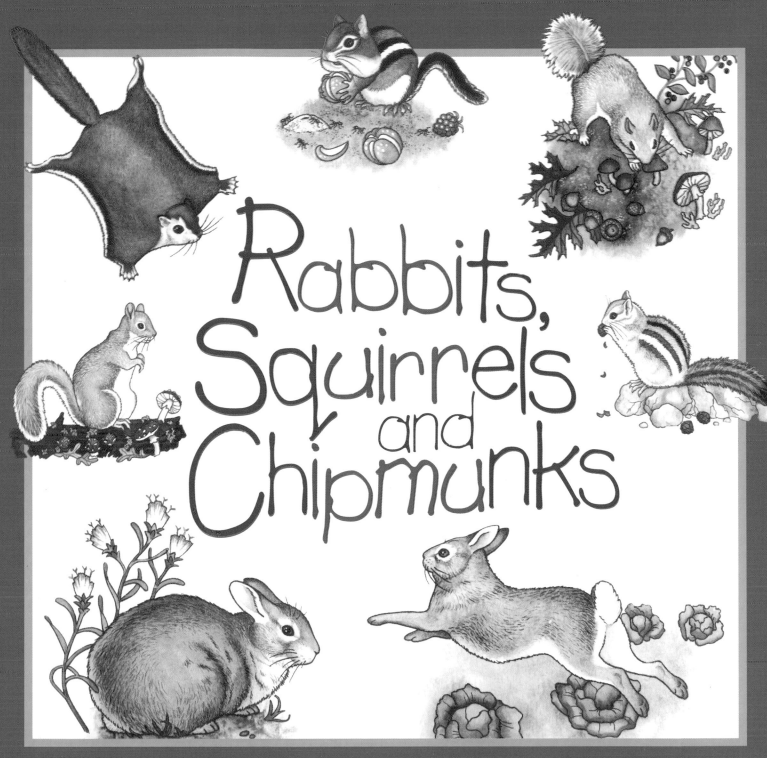

Rabbits, Squirrels and Chipmunks

by Mel Boring

illustrations by Linda Garrow

RABBITS

Rabbits may be our most popular wild animals. They are famous for their fluffy tails and big ears. Their tails are about 2 inches long and look like puff-balls. Their ears can swing in any direction to pick up the slightest sounds.

Many people think a rabbit's eyes are sharp, because they eat carrots. But rabbit eyesight is not as sharp as their hearing. Their eyes are on the sides of their heads, however, so they can see all around.

Rabbit noses help them sniff out danger. A rabbit's whiskers are long but usually light colored, so they are not very easy to see. A rabbit's back legs are longer and stronger than the front legs. Many rabbits thump their hind feet on the ground as a danger alarm.

Some rabbits are hares. What many people call the snowshoe "rabbit" is really the snowshoe hare. Jack rabbits are hares, too. Hares are bigger but skinnier than most rabbits. And hares are faster.

Most rabbits and hares do not dig burrows for homes. They scratch a shallow "bowl" out of the ground, called a form. Forms are usually hidden under bushes and trees. Rabbits spend the daytime there, going out to eat from evening to morning.

Have fun hopping into the world of rabbits!

EASTERN COTTONTAIL

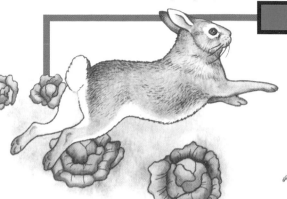

WHAT IT EATS

Eastern cottontails eat a lot of different things. They eat weeds and almost every kind of berry and fruit. When they can get into a garden they will eat the lettuce, cabbage, beans and carrots they find. But they will not dig them up.

In the winter, their favorite food is sumac. Sumac is high in fat, so it gives them body heat in cold weather.

WHAT IT LOOKS LIKE

The tail of this rabbit looks like a fluffy ball of cotton bouncing away from you. Usually the eastern cottontail hops along slowly. It also sits up on its hind legs often, to get a better view of its surroundings.

An eastern cottontail is grayish-brown above, flecked with black. It has a reddish patch on the back of its neck. Underneath, it is creamy-white. The underside of its tail is pure white. That is why it is called a "cottontail." Often this rabbit has a white spot on its forehead.

Eastern cottontails are 14 to 18 inches long, and weigh 2 to 4 pounds.

INTERESTING FACTS

Eastern cottontails can run as fast as 20 miles per hour.

WHERE TO FIND IT

Eastern cottontails live in brushy places, fields, woods and farmlands.

They can be found all over the eastern half of the United States, except New England. These cottontails also live from the Dakotas to Texas, New Mexico and Arizona.

SWAMP RABBIT

INTERESTING FACTS

The swamp rabbit is the largest rabbit in North America.

WHAT IT LOOKS LIKE

The swamp rabbit is a swimming rabbit. All rabbits can swim if they have to, but this one travels by water most of the time. To escape enemies, it ducks underwater with only its nose showing. Swamp rabbits have extra skin between their toes that helps them swim. Their big feet with spreading toes also help them walk through mud.

The swamp rabbit can be over 21 inches long. It weighs up to 6 pounds. Its fur is rough, and brown-gray with black patches. It is white underneath, with a very short, thin tail. It has reddish feet.

WHAT IT EATS

The swamp rabbit is called the "cane-cutter rabbit" in the South, because its favorite food is cane, a tall grass that grows there. It also eats sedge plant, as well as herbs that grow in water. It likes corn, too.

WHERE TO FIND IT

These rabbits live in swampy, marshy places along rivers and streams. They can be found from Georgia to eastern Texas, and from southern Indiana and Illinois along the Ohio and Mississippi rivers to the Gulf of Mexico.

MARSH RABBIT

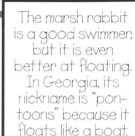

The marsh rabbit is a good swimmer, but it is even better at floating. In Georgia, its nickname is "pontoons" because it floats like a boat.

WHAT IT LOOKS LIKE

Marsh rabbits are slow runners. Walking or running, they put down one paw at a time like a cat or dog. But they can also hop and swim. A marsh rabbit gets away from its enemies by floating motionless among water plants, with its ears tucked down and just its nose and face above the water.

Marsh rabbits can also walk on just their hind legs. Most rabbits cannot do this, but the marsh rabbit does it often.

Marsh rabbits are dark red-brown, with lighter-brown tummies. They weigh about 3 1/2 pounds. Their small ears are about 2 inches long, and their tails are only about 1 1/2 inches long. The tail is brown underneath.

WHAT IT EATS

The marsh rabbit nibbles at reeds, and digs up wild potatoes and amaryllis bulbs. It also eats cane grass. In winter it eats tree leaves and twigs.

WHERE TO FIND IT

Marsh rabbits rest in brush, or in hollow logs and stumps. But they most often take shelter among tall grass and cattails in swamps.

This rabbit lives in the South, from Virginia through Florida and up to Alabama.

BRUSH RABBIT

WHAT IT LOOKS LIKE

The brush rabbit is a small, dark rabbit. It grows from 11 to 15 inches long and weighs about 1 or 2 pounds. Brush rabbits are gray-brown to brown, and speckled with black. Its tail is often shorter than 1 inch long, so you seldom see it.

"Brush" is part of the brush rabbit's name because it never hops farther than a few feet from thick, dense brush. It has shorter ears and legs than most rabbits. So it cannot hear enemies sneaking up as well and cannot run away as fast.

WHAT IT EATS

These rabbits feed mostly at night and eat herbs and grasses. One sign of brush rabbits is grass chewed down very short. Green clover is also one of their favorite meals. They eat plantain and berries, and twigs, bark and buds of Douglas fir trees in winter.

WHERE TO FIND IT

Brush rabbits do not dig burrows and rarely use the homes of other animals. Instead, brush rabbits tunnel into the dense brush.

Brush rabbits are found from Oregon's Columbia River to Baja California. They live along the western slopes of mountain ranges. They also live in cities and towns, feeding on lawns.

PYGMY RABBIT

WHAT IT EATS

Sagebrush is the pygmy rabbit's favorite food. It does not really eat much else. Sometimes it will eat a little rabbit brush.

WHAT IT LOOKS LIKE

The pygmy rabbit is the smallest rabbit of all. Less than 1 foot long, its ears are only about 2 inches long. The ears are covered with fine, silky hairs.

Their fur is peppery-brown, with light brown on their chests and legs. They have a white spot on each side of their noses. Pygmy rabbits weigh about 1 pound. Their tails are gray on top and bottom, and very short.

Unlike most other rabbits, pygmy rabbits are very social. They often live together in groups.

INTERESTING FACTS

Pygmy rabbits move close to the ground and do not hop as high as other rabbits.

WHERE TO FIND IT

The pygmy digs burrows, usually on slopes in soft, moist soil. Their burrows and tunnels go a little deeper than one yard beneath the sage and rabbit brush. Look for their small burrow doors. They are about 3 inches wide.

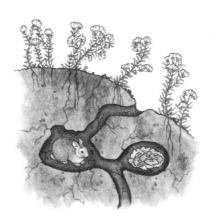

You will find pygmy rabbits in the western United States, in Montana, Idaho, Washington, Oregon, California, Nevada and Utah.

EUROPEAN RABBIT

WHAT IT EATS

When very hungry, the European rabbit will eat almost any green plant. It likes short grasses, herbs and leafy plants best.

WHERE TO FIND IT

European rabbits dig burrows. They are only active at night.

European rabbits live in brushy places and open fields. In the past 100 years they have been brought from Europe to states on the West and East Coasts. Today they can be found in many parts of the country.

WHAT IT LOOKS LIKE

The European rabbit is the most common rabbit in the world.

It is rusty brown, with white on its tummy and inside its ears. It has a creamy patch on the back of its neck. Underneath, this rabbit's tail is white. It grows 18 to 24 inches long, and weighs 3 to 5 pounds.

European rabbits are social rabbits. Some live together in large groups of over 400 rabbits! These groups have a "king" rabbit and a "queen" rabbit.

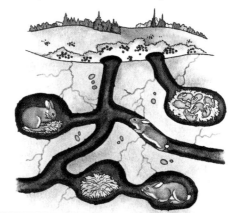

BLACK-TAILED JACK RABBIT

WHAT IT LOOKS LIKE

Though the black-tail's name says "rabbit," it is really a hare. It is the best known and most common hare.

Black-tailed jack rab-bits have very long ears, up to 6 inches long! These large rabbits can grow to be 2 feet long. They weigh as much as 8 pounds.

Sometimes black-tailed jack rabbits walk on all fours like a dog, instead of hop-ping. They have long legs and long, thick fur. Their fur is brown-gray with cream, and pep-pered with black. Underneath, they are white. Black-tails are the only hares with black on the top of their tails. The tips of their ears are also black.

WHAT IT EATS

Black-tailed jack rabbits eat at night, and rest during the day. They eat sage-brush, rabbit brush and prickly-pear cactus. They also eat mesquite, snake-weed, grama grass, greasewood, alfalfa and saltbrush. Sometimes, they eat voles.

WHERE TO FIND IT

The black-tailed jack rabbit lives from South Dakota to Washington, and from there south to Mexico. It is usually the one you see along western high-ways, especially at night, eating the grasses that grow by the roadside.

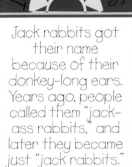

INTERESTING FACTS

Jack rabbits got their name because of their donkey-long ears. Years ago, people called them "jack-ass rabbits," and later they became just "jack rabbits."

155

WHITE-TAILED JACK RABBIT

WHAT IT EATS

White-tailed jack rabbits eat all kinds of plants, such as clover, alfalfa, filaree, spiderling and prickly pear cactus. In winter, they eat twigs, buds, bark and dried plants.

WHAT IT LOOKS LIKE

White-tailed jack rabbits wear two coats of fur, one in summer and the other in winter. During the summer, they are gray-brown. Before winter, they shed and put on a new gray or white coat. They have gray-white underparts.

The white-tailed jack rabbit's ears have black edges, which turn mostly white in winter. It has a white tail all year long.

These rabbits weigh from 5 to 9 pounds. They can grow to be 2 feet long.

This rabbit jumps over anything it has to. It could easily leap over your head! Like most hares, when the white-tailed jack rabbit is chased, it jumps straight up every few leaps to make a "spy hop" on its enemy.

WHERE TO FIND IT

These rabbits sprint around the West, from Montana to New Mexico. They can also be found from central California to Lake Michigan. They live in grassland plains and sagebrush desert.

SNOWSHOE HARE

WHAT IT EATS

Snowshoe hares eat mainly at night. They hide during the day beneath trees and come out in late afternoon. The snowshoe dines on the bark and tender tips of aspen, pine, spruce, white birch and white cedar trees. In summer, they munch grasses, clover, lupines, dandelions and strawberries.

WHAT IT LOOKS LIKE

The snowshoe hare's big feet keep it from getting stuck in the snow. When other animals bog down in snowdrifts, the snowshoe hare goes dashing through the forest. It has extra hair on its feet that keeps it from sinking, like using "snowshoes."

A snowshoe hare's fur changes color from dark brown in summer to white in winter. The tips of its ears are black in winter. Between summer and winter its fur is brown and white.

The snowshoe hare is larger than most rabbits. It weighs from 2 to 5 pounds, and grows up to 21 inches long.

WHERE TO FIND IT

Snowshoes can be found across the northern United States and in the Pacific Coast and Rocky Mountain forests, as far south as New Mexico. They can also be found in Appalachian pine forests south to Tennessee.

INTERESTING FACTS

Even if the temperature stayed warm and there was no snow on the ground, a snowshoe hare's fur would still turn white in winter.

CAPE HARE

The cape hare gives a warning noise to enemies by grating its teeth. Other hares nearby will also make the teeth-grating sound.

WHAT IT LOOKS LIKE

Cape hares are large and lanky. Some weigh over 13 pounds and grow almost 28 inches long. They have kinky fur that is brown, streaked with black. They are white beneath, with black tail-tops and black-tipped ears. In the winter, their fur is more gray than brown.

The cape hare has lots of escape tricks. It will double back on enemies chasing it and slip in behind them. It can easily leap over a 5-foot wall. It has been known to lead enemies onto ice thick enough to hold itself, but too thin for the enemies. It can even swim across wide rivers.

WHERE TO FIND IT

The cape hare can be found in New York, Vermont, New Hampshire, Massachusetts, Connecticut, Pennsylvania, New Jersey and Maryland. It is in Michigan, Wisconsin and Minnesota, too.

WHAT IT EATS

The cape hare eats grasses, herbs and fruits in summer, and switches to buds, twigs and bark in winter. Some of its summer favorites are clover, wheat, corn, berries and apples. In winter it eats the bark of apple, peach and cherry trees.

MAKE A RABBIT PAPERWEIGHT

You can make a Pygmy Rabbit or a Snowshoe Hare--or any rabbit you like--for your very own. It can be a paperweight for your desk or a decoration for your room. You can tell the sizes of the ears and the feet from the drawings in this book.

WHAT YOU NEED

- modeling clay
- pen or pencil
- stiff paper or cardboard
- scissors
- popsicle stick
- 2 pipecleaners
- 1 cottonball
- glue

WHAT TO DO

1 Shape the clay into three balls: a large one for the body, a small one for the head, and a tiny one for the nose. (Also make pieces for the feet if you want.)

2 Press the head onto the body.

3 Press the nose onto the head.

4 Draw two ears on the paper or cardboard. Cut them out. Stick them into the top of the head.

5 Draw lines for the eyes and a mouth with the popsicle stick.

6 Cut the pipecleaners into four pieces for the whiskers. Poke them in around the nose.

7 Let your rabbit harden overnight.

8 Glue the cottonball to the body for a tail.

After the rabbit is hard, you can paint it to look just like a real rabbit. If you make a large rabbit, you can put it outside to invite other rabbits to visit!

BUILD A RABBIT REFUGE

A tangled pile of brush means rabbits can find shelter and escape enemies. You can build a rabbit refuge that will keep them safe and give you the chance to see them up close. And by giving the rabbits something good to munch on, you can be sure they will keep coming back.

WHAT YOU NEED

▼

- small branches and twigs (that are less than 2 inches thick and 10 feet long), tree and hedge clippings

- Rabbit munchies:
  - clover
  - dandelions
  - carrots
  - carrot tops
  - celery
  - celery tops
  - lettuce
  - radishes
  - grass clippings

WHAT TO DO

▼

1 Pick a place where rabbits will feel safe, where there is not too much activity or noise. It should be about 10 feet wide and 10 feet long. A smaller space may also work.

2 Put the longest branches in the middle of the spot, tangling them up as much as you can. Rabbits do not like neat, tidy places, so make the branches all jumbled in a pile that fills up your space. The pile should be at least 3 feet high.

3 Poke the smaller branches and twigs into the jumbled jungle. Push enough of them in so that you cannot see the ground below the refuge. Do not be worried that rabbits will not be able to get in. They can squeeze through tiny openings, and they will want all the privacy they can get.

4 Place a few small piles of the munchies around the edges of the Rabbit Refuge. It is better not to overload them, or try to put them inside the refuge. If your piles are too deep, the food may spoil and mold at the bottom. So make your piles no deeper than about two handfuls in each spot.

Now stay away from the Rabbit Refuge, and look out through your window from time to time. If there are rabbits in your neighborhood, they will come. The best times to see them are early in the morning and near dusk. Watch for them from a safe distance at first. Later, they may feel safe enough for you to get closer to them.

SQUIRRELS

Not all squirrels are tree squirrels. Some are ground squirrels that do not climb trees. They have shorter, skinnier tails, and "talk" a lot more than tree squirrels. There is hardly a ground squirrel without a whistle, a squeak or a buzz.

Squirrels are famous for their bushy tails, and those tails come in handy. In the rain it is a squirrel's "umbrella." When it is cold, their tails are used like blankets. If they fall from a tree, their tails parachute them to a soft landing.

Ground squirrels fill their burrows with nuts and seeds for mid-winter snacks. Tree squirrels also eat nuts and seeds, but they bury them in the ground. Sometimes they forget where some nuts are buried and new trees grow.

Most squirrels are active during the day. So you might see more squirrels than any other wild animal. Wherever squirrels eat, they leave behind "crumbs" from their nutty feasts. So watch for them hopping, skipping, leaping and even flying!

GRAY SQUIRREL

WHAT IT EATS

Hickory nuts, beech-nuts, walnuts and acorns are on the gray squirrel's menu. So are seeds, corn, fruits, berries, flowers, mushrooms and caterpillars. Its favorite spring treat is sweet icicles of sap from frozen maple trees.

WHAT IT LOOKS LIKE

A gray squirrel's coat looks like it has been salted and peppered. Some black hairs and some white hairs make the whole coat look gray. The gray squirrel is bright white underneath, with tan on its ears and face. You can be sure that it is a gray squirrel if it has white-tipped hairs around its bushy tail.

This squirrel is 18 to 20 inches long including its tail. It weighs about 1 pound.

A gray squirrel can run on the ground more than 12 miles per hour, and up or down a tree almost as fast!

WHERE TO FIND IT

The gray squirrel's den is usually in a hollow part of a tree about 40 feet off the ground. They also build twiggy leaf nests, usually near their dens. They prefer shadier wooded areas. You will find lots of little holes in the ground around this squirrel's home, because they bury every nut they find in a separate hole.

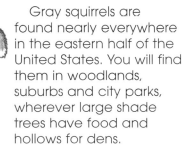

Gray squirrels are found nearly everywhere in the eastern half of the United States. You will find them in woodlands, suburbs and city parks, wherever large shade trees have food and hollows for dens.

INTERESTING FACTS

A gray squirrel's top front teeth grow about 6 inches a year, so it has to chew to keep them worn down.

163

FOX SQUIRREL

WHAT IT EATS

Acorns are a fox squirrel's favorite food. They also like hickory, beech, hazel and butternuts. Fruits and berries are food for them. And they love corn on the cob. They even eat cherry seeds, plum stones and thornapple pits.

You can tell which nuts have been eaten by fox squirrels. They tear the shells to pieces. Other squirrels gnaw a hole in one or both ends of the shell to get the nut out.

WHERE TO FIND IT

Fox squirrels prefer a hollow in an oak or hickory tree to live in. You will find fox squirrels in the eastern half of the United States, except in New England. Some fox squirrels live in the West Coast states, from Washington to California. In the South, they live in cypress and mangrove swamps, and places with pine trees.

WHAT IT LOOKS LIKE

The fox squirrel is as red as a fox in the North. That is how it got its name. It also has a bushy tail like a fox. This squirrel is the largest of all tree squirrels. It grows 18 to 29 inches long and weighs from 1 to 3 pounds.

In some states fox squirrels are as gray as gray squirrels. In the South, this squirrel is black and often has a white nose and tail-tip. You can tell a fox squirrel by its large size. It also has yellowish tips on its tail hairs.

RED SQUIRREL

WHAT IT LOOKS LIKE

This little squirrel has a loud voice. It looks like it is dressed in a rusty red coat and gray-white vest. During the summer, a black side stripe separates the red from the white. Its tail matches its coat, with a wide black border frosted with white. The red squirrel has a white eye ring that stands out brightly.

Red squirrels are less than 16 inches long, nose to tail-tip, and weigh about 1/2 pound.

WHAT IT EATS

Red squirrels eat seeds from tulip, sycamore, maple and elm trees, plus hickory nuts and acorns. They are also very fond of mushrooms. But spruce cone seeds are their favorite.

These squirrels do not just use the seeds from the cones. They also make nests in underground burrows using cone scraps. Red squirrels prefer tree-hollow dens or leaf nests about 40 feet up in the trees.

WHERE TO FIND IT

Red squirrels live in any kind of forest with pine trees, hardwood trees, or both. Often, they live near buildings.

They can be found in the Rocky Mountain states, from Canada to Arizona and New Mexico. They also live in the Midwest, from Iowa to Ohio. And in the East, from Maine south to Georgia.

DOUGLAS' SQUIRREL

WHAT IT EATS

The Douglas' squirrel likes pine cone seeds best. It climbs high and cuts down green pine cones. Those it does not eat, it stores in damp places under logs, stumps or rocks, where they keep for 2 or 3 years. It also eats nuts and berries. Sometimes the Douglas' wedges mushrooms in tree forks to dry, then eats them later.

WHAT IT LOOKS LIKE

The Douglas' is one of the smallest tree squirrels, only 10 to 14 inches long. It weighs just over 1/2 pound. And this little squirrel is the most rowdy of all squirrels. It may drop 5-pound pine cones from 150 feet high onto a camper's tent!

The Douglas' squirrel is dark red-brown on its back, with rusty yellow undersides. Along each side, a black line separates its brown back from its yellowish belly. In winter, it grows small tufts of black hair on its ears. Its tail has a whitish fringe.

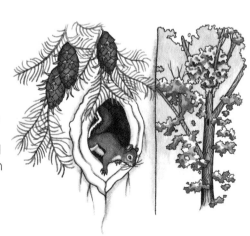

WHERE TO FIND IT

This squirrel likes to nest in a fir tree hole. But it also builds twig-and-leaf nests high up in pine trees. The nest looks like a big ball of leaves.

Douglas' squirrels can be found in the northwestern United States in Washington, Oregon, and south into California in tall pines and spruces.

ABERT'S SQUIRREL

WHAT IT LOOKS LIKE

The Abert's is the best-dressed squirrel in the West. It looks like it is wearing a white vest and white, fluffy tails. The long, black hairs on its head in winter look like a "top hat."

An Abert's squirrel weighs about 2 pounds, and is around 20 inches long. Its back is reddish-brown, and its sides are gray. Its tail is gray-white on top, with white underneath.

On the ground, Abert's squirrels carry their tails in a question-mark curve. They look clumsy when they walk, but they can run in smooth leaps along the ground.

WHAT IT EATS

Abert's squirrels eat acorns, seeds, berries and fungus. But its main food is the inner bark of ponderosa pine trees. It also eats spikenard roots and mistletoe.

INTERESTING FACTS

Abert's squirrels are very patient. Hiding from predators, they can lie still without twitching a tail hair for up to 2 hours.

WHERE TO FIND IT

The ponderosa pine is home for the Abert's. It builds a leaf nest on a twiggy platform, as wide as 3 feet. The nest's sturdy walls keep out winter's chill.

Abert's squirrels live in the southern Rocky Mountains. They can be found In Colorado and Utah, New Mexico, and around the Grand Canyon of Arizona.

KAIBAB SQUIRREL

WHAT IT LOOKS LIKE

Kaibabs are tassel-eared squirrels. Tufts of hair up to 2 inches long grow on their ears in the winter and stay until June, then they are shed. Kaibabs are about 19 to 21 inches long, and weigh 1 1/2 to 2 pounds. This squirrel is dark brown-gray all over, except for its snow-white tail.

Kaibab squirrels are very shy, and not nearly as noisy as other squirrels. You might walk under a tree where a Kaibab is without knowing it, because it keeps quiet.

At first glance, because of its black-and-white coloring, a Kaibab is often mistaken for a skunk. But kaibabs walk along gracefully, while skunks move with an awkward waddle.

WHAT IT EATS

Kaibabs feed on the soft inner bark of the ponderosa pines where they live. They eat mushrooms that grow under the needles covering the forest floor. They open apples just to get the seeds. Acorns, berries and roots are also Kaibab food.

WHERE TO FIND IT

Kaibab squirrels live only on a mountaintop across the Grand Canyon from Abert's squirrels. The plateau they live on towers 9,000 feet high. They live in the forests up there and cannot get down.

Kaibab squirrels build twig-and-needle nests, sometimes 89 feet up in the fork of a pine tree.

FLYING SQUIRREL

The longest glide of a flying squirrel ever measured was 300 feet. That is as long as a football field!

WHAT IT LOOKS LIKE

The flying squirrel only comes out after dark. This "flyer" does not really fly. It spreads the folds of skin that connect its front and back legs and glides like a kite on the wind in perfect silence.

Flying squirrels always land lower than where they take off. So they must climb up again for the next glide. Doing this, they can still go farther and faster than a person can keep up on the ground.

The northern flying squirrel is about 1 foot long. Its fur is a rich tan to cinnamon-brown, with dull white undersides. The southern flying squirrel is only 8 to 10 inches long. It is silky gray-brown, and creamy-white underneath.

WHAT IT EATS

Flying squirrels fuel their flight by eating bugs, acorns, hickory nuts, cherries and sunflower seeds. They also eat sugar maple blossoms, pine berries, lichens and bark. One flying squirrel family can eat a quart of June bugs in one meal.

WHERE TO FIND IT

Either the northern or southern flying squirrel can be found in every state except Colorado, New Mexico and Arizona. They make their dens in hollow trees, often in old woodpecker nests. They also build leaf nests.

Flying squirrels also have been known to move into bird houses, garages, attics, chimneys and mailboxes.

ROCK SQUIRREL

WHAT IT LOOKS LIKE

Rock squirrels are twice as long and twice as heavy as most ground squirrels. They grow up to 21 inches long and are as heavy as 2 pounds.

A rock squirrel does climb trees, but mostly it climbs around rocks. Its peppered, gray-brown fur helps it hide among those rocks. Its tail is brown and white. Its ears are smaller than most tree squirrels' ears.

INTERESTING FACTS

Rock squirrels got their name because they love to sit and sunbathe on the rocks.

WHAT IT EATS

Rock squirrels love to eat piñon nuts and acorns. They gobble up fig, cactus and wild gourd seeds, juniper berries, apricots and peaches. Rock squirrels eat seeds out of watermelons, and dig up newly planted corn. They also pounce on grasshoppers and earthworms.

WHERE TO FIND IT

A rock squirrel tries to make the door to its burrow between rocks so the door cannot be chewed bigger by enemies. Because of this, the squirrel does not have to hide its door like other ground squirrels do. It just leaves its dug-out dirt piled by the door. Sometimes the pile of dirt is enough to fill a barrel!

Rock squirrels can be found in the desert Southwest. They live from Oklahoma west to Nevada and California, and from Utah and Colorado south to Arizona, New Mexico and Texas.

THIRTEEN-LINED GROUND SQUIRREL

WHAT IT LOOKS LIKE

The thirteen-lined ground squirrel looks like it has a little flag on its back, with 13 stripes and spots that look like stars. These ground squirrels are brown, with light and dark brown stripes and light brown spots and undersides.

A thirteen-lined ground squirrel grows about 11 inches long. It weighs about 1/2 pound. When it comes out of hibernation in April, it weighs half as much as it did in October.

WHAT IT EATS

The thirteen-lined eats a wide variety of foods. Oats, wheat, beans, sunflower seeds, cottonseed, goosefoot, knotweed and buffalo-bur are part of its diet. It also eats crickets, ants, beetles, wireworms, June bug grubs and butterflies. It likes frogs and even mice too. Grasshoppers are their favorite snack.

WHERE TO FIND IT

Thirteen-lined ground squirrels can be found all over the middle of the United States from Canada to Texas, and Utah to Ohio.

INTERESTING FACTS

The thirteen-lined ground squirrel really has about 23 stripes. But some are just broken lines that look like lines of spots.

Look for it on golf courses and along roadsides, in most any mowed grass. It is often seen standing by its burrow, straight as a tent stake, front paws tight against its chest. If it senses danger, it will dive underground, then poke its nose out and make a bird-like noise.

GOLDEN-MANTLED GROUND SQUIRREL

WHAT IT LOOKS LIKE

This ground squirrel looks like a chipmunk, but it is bigger. One sure way to recognize it is by the reddish-brown "golden cape" around its head and shoulders. Also, it does not have face stripes like a chipmunk. The golden has a white stripe on each side between two black stripes, and yellowish-white tummy. Gray-brown fur covers its back and lower sides.

Above and below the eyes of a golden-mantled ground squirrel is a bright white crescent. Together, the crescents look like a ring around each eye.

The golden-mantled grows from 9 to 12 inches long. It is 3 times as heavy as most chipmunks. Most ground squirrels have tiny ears, but this one has large, rounded ears.

WHAT IT EATS

Fruits, seeds and nuts are this ground squirrel's main foods. A few of their favorite fruits are strawberries, cherries, Oregon grapes and thimbleberries. They also eat the seeds of yellow pine, Douglas fir and silver pine trees.

WHERE TO FIND IT

This ground squirrel is found on pine mountain slopes, among rocks and fallen trees. They are in every state west of a line down through Montana, Wyoming, Colorado and New Mexico.

HANG A SQUIRREL NUT-BALL

Squirrels love all kinds of nuts. If you hang up a squirrel nut-ball, you will have fun watching them try to catch it—and maybe even swing from it! Don't worry if they pull it down—that's fun too!

WHAT YOU NEED

▼

- All the nuts you can find. It is better if they are in the shell. But shelled peanuts—and even kernels of corn—will also work.

- peanut butter

- wax paper

- a piece of thin wire about 12 inches long

- a piece of string or cord 5 feet long

WHAT TO DO

▼

1 Roll the nuts in a thin coat of peanut butter. Place each nut on the wax paper.

2 Make little balls of nuts by sticking smaller nuts together. Bigger nuts do not need to be stuck to others just yet.

3 When you have about ten big nut clusters, stick them all together in one big ball. The nut-ball should be about 6 inches across.

4 Set the ball aside on the wax paper for a couple days to let it harden.

5 Push the wire through the center of the nut-ball, so half is sticking out on each side. Twist the ends of the wire together.

6 Tie one end of the string to the wire loop.

7 Tie the other end of the string to the branch of a tree. Make sure the ball hangs so it is not resting against the tree trunk, but will swing in all directions.

CHIPMUNKS

It may surprise you that chipmunks are also ground squirrels, a special kind. It is difficult even for animal experts to tell the many kinds of chipmunks apart. Some look as alike as twins. The best way to tell what kind of chipmunk you see is by where you are, because almost every kind of chipmunk lives in its own separate area.

All chipmunks have stripes on their faces. They are lighter than other ground squirrels. They weigh from about 1 ounce to 5 ounces. If a chipmunk is said to be brown-gray, it is because that kind will be browner in summer, grayer in winter. In dry deserts, chipmunk colors will be lighter, and stripes less clear. In sunnier, open forests, colors will be brighter, and stripes easier to see.

Chipmunks have pouches opening in the back corners of their mouths. The pouches run down along both sides of their necks. They carry their food in these pouches.

Chipmunks hibernate in burrows in winter, but not like bears. They deep-sleep, but wake up every few days to eat.

The sound chipmunks make is usually a "chip, chip," from which their name comes. But it may sound like "chuck" or "chock."

Chipmunks scamper and scurry about in the daytime. They are fun to watch as they look for nuts and other goodies!

EASTERN CHIPMUNK

WHAT IT EATS

The eastern always seems to be looking for food. It stores most of it in its burrow for its long winter sleep.

A list of every food the eastern eats and stores would fill this whole page. It likes all kinds of seeds, nuts, berries and fruits. They love flowers like the star flower, bugs like millipedes and ants, and frogs.

WHAT IT LOOKS LIKE

The eastern chipmunk has a wide, dark center stripe down its back. On each side it has a white stripe between 2 black stripes. That equals 7 stripes in all on its back and sides. The side stripes run from its neck to its behind, which is reddish. This chipmunk is 8 to 12 inches long. It weighs 2 to 4 ounces.

Eastern chipmunks usually run with their tails straight out behind them, unlike some other chipmunks that run with their tails pointing straight up.

To unload acorns from their cheek pouches, eastern chipmunks squeeze their cheeks with their front paws and out pop the acorns!

WHERE TO FIND IT

The eastern chipmunk is found in the eastern half of the United States. It lives along the edges of oak, hickory, maple and beech woodlands. Easterns dig burrow systems up to 30 feet long and 3 feet underground.

TOWNSEND'S CHIPMUNK

WHAT IT LOOKS LIKE

Townsend's chipmunks are the darkest-colored of all chipmunks. They are dark red-brown, and even their light stripes are not very white. The edges of its stripes are not as clear as most chipmunks' and its dark stripes are brown rather than crisp black. It has 9 stripes in all.

They grow between 9 and 11 inches long and can weigh up to 3 ounces. You can tell a Townsend's chipmunk by the bright red fur on the underside of its tail.

WHAT IT EATS

The Townsend's eats nuts, seeds and berries. In summer, it gulps down many kinds of berries. By fall, it switches to acorns, maple seeds and pine cone seeds. A special treat for a Townsend's is hazelnuts.

WHERE TO FIND IT

Townsend's chipmunks do not always live on the ground. This big chipmunk's nest of sedge and lichen is usually under a tree stump, but is sometimes in a tree.

A Townsend's chipmunk's burrow is usually under yellow pine, redwood, hemlock or fir trees. They live in Washington and Oregon, west of the Cascade Mountains. They are in northern California, too, along the Pacific Ocean, and down into the Sierra Mountains into Nevada.

MERRIAM'S CHIPMUNK

WHAT IT LOOKS LIKE

The stripes of the Merriam's chipmunk do not stand out as brightly as other chipmunks' stripes. Its sides are gray, and so are all its light stripes. The dark stripes are brown. The stripes on its head are 3 grays plus 2 browns. It has dull black spots at the eye corners, and a gray-white tummy.

The Merriam's chipmunk grows to be about 11 inches long. About half of that length is the tail. It has a longer tail than other chipmunks. This chipmunk can weigh about 2 to 4 ounces.

WHAT IT EATS

Merriam's chipmunks like to eat the small piñon pine nuts. They eat fruits like juniper berries, and seeds from the blue lupine. Merriam's chipmunks also munch the flowers and leaves of shrubs such as the manzanita.

WHERE TO FIND IT

It makes a nest about the size and shape of a coconut in its burrow. The burrow is dug under the stump of a ponderosa, yellow or digger pine tree. This chipmunk can be found in the brush and woodlands of the southwest quarter of California, from San Francisco to Mexico.

INTERESTING FACTS

Merriam's chipmunks have been found as high as 70 or 80 feet up in pine trees. They can climb even higher than the red squirrel.

CLIFF CHIPMUNK

WHAT IT LOOKS LIKE

This chipmunk is a cliff-climber, and uses its tail to steer itself. If it falls, it twirls its tail like a tiny helicopter and lands softly.

The cliff chipmunk has a gray coat, with touches of brown, and gray-white patches behind its ears. Its bright white face stripes sometimes stand out. The black stripe down the middle of its back is its boldest dark stripe, but it is not always clear. The stripes on its sides are often blurry, too. One tell-tale sign of a cliff chipmunk is the rust-red beneath its tail.

Cliff chipmunks are medium-sized chipmunks, between 8 and 11 inches long. They weigh 2 to 3 ounces.

WHAT IT EATS

Cliff chipmunks feast on piñon nuts and juniper berries. They also eat grass seeds, insects and bird eggs. In dry times, they eat juicy cactus fruit.

WHERE TO FIND IT

Cliff chipmunks live in rocky mountains and canyons in Oregon, Idaho, Wyoming, Nevada, Utah, Colorado, Arizona and New Mexico. You can see them in Grand Canyon and Zion national parks.

Their burrows may be underground, or they may use cracks in the cliffside with nests of dried grass.

INTERESTING FACTS

A cliff chipmunk sways its tail back and forth to send an alarm, unlike the flicking, up-and-down tail motions that most chipmunks use.

UINTA CHIPMUNK

WHAT IT EATS

The Uinta eats mostly nuts, seeds and fruits. Piñon pine nuts, yellow-pine seeds and juniper berries are its usual meals.

WHAT IT LOOKS LIKE

Uinta chipmunks live where winter is cold, so they hibernate longer than most western chipmunks. To carry in enough food for winter, it uses its inner chipmunk cheeks like shopping carts.

A Uinta chipmunk is gray on the top of its head and behind its neck. It has two black spots at its eye corners that look almost like a stripe. Uintas have gray hips and reddish sides. The lowest side stripe is pure white and the dark stripes are blackish.

Their tails are grayish-black, and their tummies are creamy-white. Uintas grow to be 8 or 9 inches long and can be as heavy as 2 to 3 ounces.

WHERE TO FIND IT

Uintas live high in mountain spots in parts of Wyoming, Colorado, Utah, Nevada, Idaho and Montana. A few can also be found in Arizona and California.

LODGEPOLE CHIPMUNK

WHERE TO FIND IT

Look for this climbing chipmunk around and in lodgepole pines, where those straight-trunk trees grow close together. Often, manzanita bushes will be near a lodgepole's burrow.

The lodgepole chipmunk is found in central California and in Nevada at the bend in its western border.

Lodgepole chipmunks like to live on the west sides of mountains where the ground is wetter.

WHAT IT LOOKS LIKE

The top of a lodgepole's head and neck are bright brown in summer and its sides are rust-red. Its lowest light side stripe is very white, and is wider than the other light stripes. Its dark and light stripes stand out like a zebra's.

A lodgepole is about as long and heavy as an ear of corn-on-the-cob. It is about 7 to 9 inches long.

WHAT IT EATS

Manzanita bushes make a two-course meal for lodgepoles, because they eat both the flowers and the berries. They also eat small nuts like piñons and fungus. Caterpillars are eaten, too, but usually only when there is not much other food.

YELLOW-PINE CHIPMUNK

WHAT IT EATS

The yellow-pine's handy "hands" easily pick the seeds out of strawberries and goose-berries. It eats mostly seeds, plus fruits, buds and fungi like mushrooms.

Yellow-pine chipmunks are not such eager nut-eaters as other chipmunks. These chipmunks love seeds, and it does not matter if they are ripe or still green. They eat the seeds of knotweed, yarrow, larch, thistle, huckleberry and yellow-pine trees.

WHAT IT LOOKS LIKE

The lightest and brightest chipmunk of all is the yellow-pine chipmunk. Some even·say its brown-red sides are cinna-mon-pink. The yellow-pine has stripes that stand out clearly on its face and body as well.

This chipmunk grows no longer than 10 inches, and weighs up to 2 1/2 ounces. A yellow-pine is yellow-white on its underparts, and the underneath of its tail is a brown-yellow.

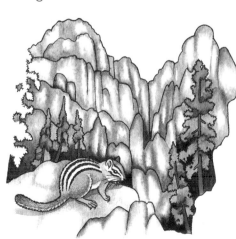

WHERE TO FIND IT

Yellow-pines live east of the Cascade Mountains in Washington and Oregon, and along the eastern slope of the Sierra Nevada Mountains in California, over into Nevada. These bright chipmunks add color to the Rocky Mountains in Idaho, Montana, Wyoming and Utah.

LEAST CHIPMUNK

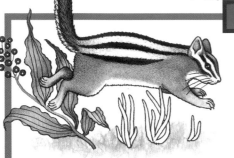

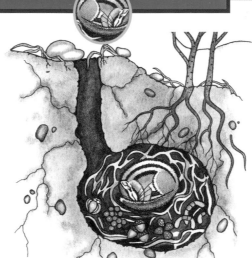

WHAT IT LOOKS LIKE

As its name says, the least chipmunk is little. A newborn least is only as big as a thimble. Most leasts are under 9 inches long. They always run with their tails up.

The colors of a least chipmunk's sides vary from orange-brown to dark gray, and it comes in more different colors than any other chipmunk. Unlike other chipmunks, the least's middle black back stripe runs from head to tail. Their tummies are gray-white.

WHAT IT EATS

Least chipmunks love berries, but they leave the pulp and take only the seeds. Blueberries, raspberries, strawberries and thimbleberries are their favorites. In spring, they eat grasshoppers, beetles and caterpillars.

WHERE TO FIND IT

Least chipmunks are excellent climbers, and may even nest in a tree, or just sun themselves on a branch.

Least chipmunks are found in more places than any other western chipmunk. They burrow into sagebrush desert and high mountains from North Dakota south to New Mexico, west through Arizona to California, and north to Washington. They also scamper through pine forests in Michigan, Wisconsin and Minnesota.

INTERESTING FACTS

In summer, least chipmunks may live in abandoned woodpecker holes or sleep in a tree nest of leaves.

ALPINE CHIPMUNK

WHAT IT LOOKS LIKE

The alpine chipmunk is the tiniest chipmunk of all. It is only about 6 to 8 inches long. Its long, fuzzy fur always looks like it needs combing.

An alpine chipmunk is brownish-yellow to gray. Its stripes are paler than any other chipmunk's stripes. It is gray on top of its head, with gray-white patches behind its ears. Its dark stripes are reddish or brownish.

You can spot an alpine by the light orange on the underside of its black-tipped tail. The alpine's tail is more flat than round.

WHAT IT EATS

Foods for the alpine chipmunk are nuts, pine seeds and berries. It also eats insects. Sometimes it will eat bird eggs. Unlike most chipmunks, alpines put on a lot of fat in late summer, to prepare for the cold mountain winter where they live.

WHERE TO FIND IT

Alpines live in the Sierra Mountains of east-central California, in an area only about 195 miles long and 25 miles wide. You may see this chipmunk if you visit Yosemite, King's Canyon or Sequoia national parks. They climb among rocks that have fallen from cliffs.

WATCH THE CHIPMUNKS WALK A TIGHTROPE

Chipmunks are curious little animals. They can learn simple tasks that will give you hours of fun, and them hours of food—or hours of figuring out how to get to the food, anyway.

WHAT YOU NEED

- 6 peanuts in their shells

- 6 pieces of string, each cut 8 inches long

- a clothesline, or a rope tied between two trees about 5 feet off the ground

WHAT TO DO

1 Tie one end of each string around the middle of a peanut.

2 Tie the other end of each string to the clothesline or rope. Tie the peanuts to the line so they are at least 1 foot apart.

3 Watch your tightrope from a distance that the chipmunks will be comfortable with.

After the chipmunks have found the peanuts by smell, they will have to become high-wire walkers to get them. They will climb the clothesline pole or tree, and make their way to the rope. Then they will carefully try to walk to the peanut string. They will probably try to untie the string from the peanut!

MAKE A CHIPMUNK SWIMMING POOL

Some animals swim regularly, even some rab-bits. Most all animals can swim, if they have to. And if you set up a swimming pool for the chipmunks, they will want to swim. Just make sure the pool is not deep.

WHAT YOU NEED

- a shallow, flat-bottomed bowl, basin or tub (at least 18 inches across and no deeper than 4 inches)

- a garden hoe or shovel

- water from a hose or bucket

- a peanut in the shell, or another type of nut that floats

WHAT TO DO

1 Pick a spot on the ground where you want to set the swimming pool. Put it near where you have seen chipmunks.

2 Using the hoe or edge of the shovel, scrape the ground a little so that the bowl will not wobble.

3 Put about 2 or 3 inches of water in the bowl.

4 Let it stay there for a day or two, so that the chipmunks get used to it. They might even try to drink from it.

5 After a day or so, float a peanut in the bowl. Then go away and watch from a distance.

The chipmunks will want the peanut, and even swim for it. Some chipmunks will even take a "bath" to get the peanut. After you have floated a few, and the chipmunks have gone swimming for them, you might even hear them scolding you if you forget to fill the pool, or forget to put peanuts in it!

SCRAPBOOK

Rabbits, Squirrels and Chipmunks

Tracks, Scats and Signs

by Leslie Dendy

illustrations by Linda Garrow

INTRODUCTION

There are many wild animals in fields and forests and ponds. Some of them are easy to see. But a lot of them are hard to find.

Wild animals leave clues everywhere they go. They dig underground tunnels. They make footprints in snow or mud. They chew plants along the way, and poop in their paths. They build nests. Their feathers and fur and dried skins fall off.

Be careful when you look for clues. Many of them blend in with the ground and the plants. You can bring a pencil and use the blank pages at the back of this book to draw what you see. A magnifying glass is fun to bring along also. You can use the ruler on the back of this book to measure what you find. The more time you spend looking for them, the more clues you will discover.

TRACKS

Animal footprints are called tracks. It's easy to find tracks in the snow. You can also find them in soft or muddy places when you walk along a path or dirt road. Look at the mud along the edges of streams, rivers, and ponds. Look in the sand at the beach, too.

Hunt for tracks that show clear toe prints. Count the toes and look at their shapes. Look for tiny dots made by the animal's claws.

Be sure to notice the size of the tracks. Squirrels and raccoons both make tracks that look like little hands, but raccoon tracks are two or three times bigger.

SCATS

Dogs poop on lawns, and people hurry to clean it up. Wild animal poop is another story. It even tells a story—about which animal came by and what it had eaten.

Scientists call the poop "scat." They call small pieces "droppings" or "scats." Scats come in many shapes and sizes. Most of them are not stinky.

Scats contain pieces of food that the animal could not digest. Rabbit droppings contain tiny pieces of twigs and leaves. Skunk scat is packed with insect bodies and wings. Fox scat may be full of mouse fur and bones one day, and blueberry or apple skins another day.

Look for scat near an animal's tracks or near its nest. You can use a stick to break it apart to see what is in it.

SIGNS

Wild animals leave many other clues about their busy lives besides tracks and scats. All the clues are called signs. A sign is anything you see that tells you where an animal has been and what it was doing. When an owl eats mice, moles, or voles, it digests the meat. Then it spits up a hard brown blob called a "pellet." It's full of fur and tiny bones and skulls.

Spiders let out liquid silk, which hardens into shiny threads. They use some threads as safety lines, like a rock climber's ropes. They also make webs to catch insects. Then they wrap some insects in tiny silk packages before they bite them.

A bird has thousands of feathers, and they fall off sometimes so new ones can grow. If you find a big pile of feathers, the bird was probably killed by a cat or a hawk. Or you can look for bird droppings on leaves.

Some wasps chew wood into tiny pieces to make paper. They build a tiny paper room for each baby, and wrap more paper around the outside.

These are just some of the signs you can look for to help identify which animals have been in the area.

BE SMART AND SAFE

Woods and other wild places are great fun, but they are wild. You probably won't be chased by a bear, but you could get bitten by a tick or a snake if you are not careful. You could get sunburned or bump into poison ivy. Always go with a grownup who knows the dangers in your area.

Here are three rules that wildlife scientists use to stay safe:

1   Don't touch wild animals. They are normally shy and afraid of people. If a wild animal lets you get close, it is probably sick or injured. It could bite. Leave it alone and call the animal experts. Also, never touch baby animals or birds. Just because you do not see the parents nearby does not mean the babies are alone. Touching them may make the parents angry and dangerous.

2   Don't eat wild plants or berries, unless a plant expert tells you it will not hurt you.

3   Don't touch animal nests or scats with your bare hands. They may contain bacteria, fleas, or other pests that could make you sick.

THE FOREST

For the animals that live in a forest, the trees and bushes are not just scenery. They are houses and food. Animals drill holes in the trunk or build nests in the branches. They gobble leaves, fruits, and nuts. They bite off the bark. They even eat the dead leaves and pine needles on the ground.

Look at the plants from top to bottom. You might see bear claw marks marching up a tree trunk. Down below, snails and slugs make their own slippery, slimy sidewalks across leaves and logs.

Leaves are like lettuce for caterpillars and grasshoppers, grubs, and slugs. Some chew big holes or tiny tunnels. Others suck the sugary leaf juice and make the leaves shrivel. Many butterflies, moths, and bugs hide their tiny, bead-like eggs on the bottoms of leaves. Then the hungry birds won't find them. But you can when you know what to look for!

RABBITS

Rabbits hop around hunting for plants to eat. And they hop in a hurry to escape enemies like owls and foxes.

Rabbit tracks are especially easy to see in the snow. When a rabbit hops, its four feet land in a clump shaped like a Y or a V.

Rabbit scats are hard balls, the size of peas or marbles. If you find a lot, the rabbit probably stopped there to eat. Look for branches that were bitten off with a diagonal cut.

A rabbit nest is like a bowl in the ground. It may be hidden under a bush. When a mother has babies, she puts grass and some of her fur inside the nest for them.

WOODPECKERS

What pecks all those holes in tree trunks? Woodpeckers, of course.

Hidden under the tree bark, many beetles and ants are chewing tunnels in the wood and laying their eggs. Woodpeckers can hear the insects chewing.

A woodpecker hammers its beak into the bark to make a hole. Its long tongue reaches through the tunnels and—zap!—grabs a snack.

Woodpeckers make bigger holes for nests.
The mother bird puts small wood chips in the hole, and
lays her eggs on them.

Many other animals borrow woodpecker holes
later. If you find one, it could have squirrels or owls or
raccoons inside.

SQUIRRELS

Squirrels leave their lunch leftovers on the ground. They drop empty acorns near oak trees. They chomp holes in hickory nuts and leave the shells behind. They also tear apart pine cones to eat the tasty seeds hidden inside.

You may also find a pile of little branches under a tree. Squirrels bite off small branches, so they can get the pine cones or tender buds at the end. They drop the rest of the branch to the ground.

Some squirrels make round nests as big as basketballs in the tree-tops. They build the nests with twigs, leaves, grass, or bark. Other squirrels live in old woodpecker holes.

Squirrel tracks look almost like doll hands. Look for them along a muddy road, or scampering across the snow from tree to tree.

PORCUPINES

A prickly porcupine can stab an enemy with its 30,000 quills. It doesn't need to run away fast. It waddles like a duck, and its tail drags on the ground. The quills make brush marks in the dust or snow.

When snow is deep, a porcupine just plows through, making a wavy ditch.

Porcupines climb trees to get tender twigs, buds, or acorns. They drop acorn shells and bitten-off branches under the tree. Some trees have huge bare spots where porcupines have pulled off the bark and eaten it.

Porcupine scats are shaped like peanuts or cashew nuts. They may be connected like a necklace.

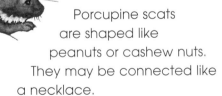

DEER

Many times you will only see deer as they leap away to hide. But you can see their lumpy paths through the forest, and their tracks.

A deer foot has two big toes with curved hooves. The toes may spread apart—or stay close together, making footprints like hearts. If the foot sinks into snow or mud, two more tiny toes may show.

Deer leave piles of brown droppings near their paths, shaped like grapes or bullets.

When a deer nibbles trees and shrubs, the chewed ends look rough. This is because a deer has no top front teeth. It rips a branch with its bottom teeth and lips. Deer also bite strips of bark off trees.

A deer "bed" is a mashed-down place in snow or grass, as big as a sled.

VISIT A ROTTEN LOG HOTEL

When a tree dies, it rots slowly. The wood gets softer. Animals dig and chew little "rooms" inside it, where they can stay safe and be warm in the winter. Even after they move out, you can see the signs they left behind.

It's fun to pick apart a rotten log or stump with a pocket knife or stick. You can make a list of the animals and signs you find, and you can draw them on the blank pages at the back of this book.

1 First kick the log gently, to scare away any snakes that may be hiding inside. If the log is damp, you may see slime trails of snails or slugs on it.

2 Peel off a strip of loose bark. There could be a caterpillar or salamander underneath. You may see tiny tunnels, chewed by beetles and ants.

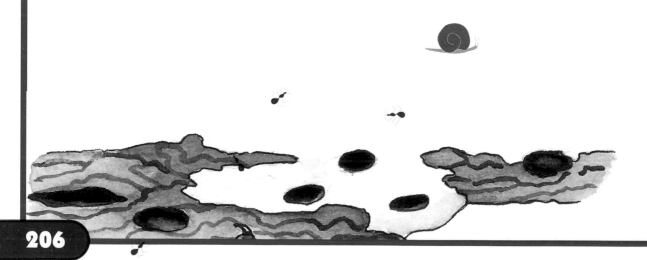

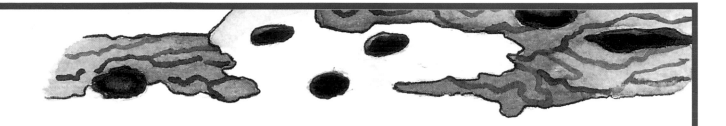

3 Pick apart the crumbly wood. Centipedes, millipedes, spiders, or sow bugs may run and hide. Look for insect nests full of eggs or wormy larvae. Be careful. Only touch the wood.

4 If the log is hollow, you might find a chipmunk nest or a snakeskin inside. There may be a pile of nuts and acorns saved by a squirrel. There may be snake or lizard eggs under the log.

Be sure you leave most of the log as you found it, so the animals can come back to their home!

THE FIELD

Grasshoppers and butterflies are easy to find in a field, but many animals are hiding. Look for paths mashed down in the grass.

Hunt for little piles of dirt. These mounds could mark the "door" to the home of a dirt-digger, like a badger or a woodchuck.

Watch ants carrying food to their nest along tiny trails. The ants can smell their way. They make trails by dotting chemicals on the ground with their tail-ends.

Look closely at the plants. You may find a funnel-shaped spider web or a pile of grass pieces chewed by a mouse.

FOXES

Finding a fox is tricky business. But you can find fox tracks trotting through a field or forest.

A fox paw print has four toes with claw marks. A fox often walks in a straight line. Its rear feet step in the same spots as its front feet. This makes a neat dotted line. If you see sloppier tracks wandering around, they probably were made by a dog.

A fox family often lives in a burrow that was dug by a woodchuck or badger. The "front door" hole is as wide as a soccer ball. When the foxes kick dirt out of the den, it makes a big pile on one side. You may find fox leftovers on the pile, such as feathers, bones, or mouse fur.

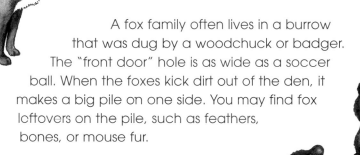

SKUNKS

Your nose knows when a skunk is near. A skunk can squirt stinky spray in an enemy's face. The smell can tell you where to look for more signs—if you dare!

You might find the skunk's sleeping place. It could be a hole in the ground or under a building.

Skunk scat is dark and chunky. Poke it with a stick. It may be full of bee wings or plant seeds or mouse fur. And you can guess what the skunk was eating.

Skunks have long claws for digging up mouse and bee nests in the ground. You may find the holes where a skunk dug. And you can see little claw dots in their footprints.

COYOTES

If coyotes live nearby, you may be wakened by their howling songs and barks in the middle of the night.

Coyotes run long distances in fields or forests, often along human trails. In the snow, the tracks go on and on. They often make a straight dotted line, like fox tracks. A coyote paw print is oval with four toes and two middle claw dots. A rounder print with spread-apart toes could be a dog's print.

Coyote scats are the size of fat hot dogs. Like fox droppings, they may be full of fruit in the summer, or mouse hairs and bones in other seasons.

SNAKES

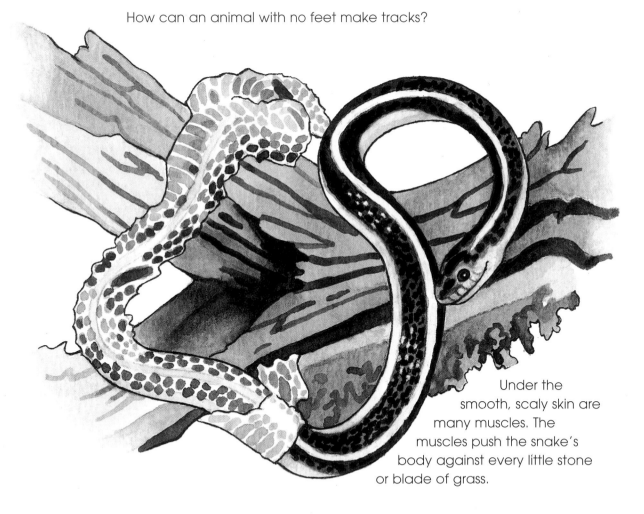

A snake can slide between the blades of grass and sneak up on a frog. It can slither into a mouse tunnel.

How can an animal with no feet make tracks?

Under the smooth, scaly skin are many muscles. The muscles push the snake's body against every little stone or blade of grass.

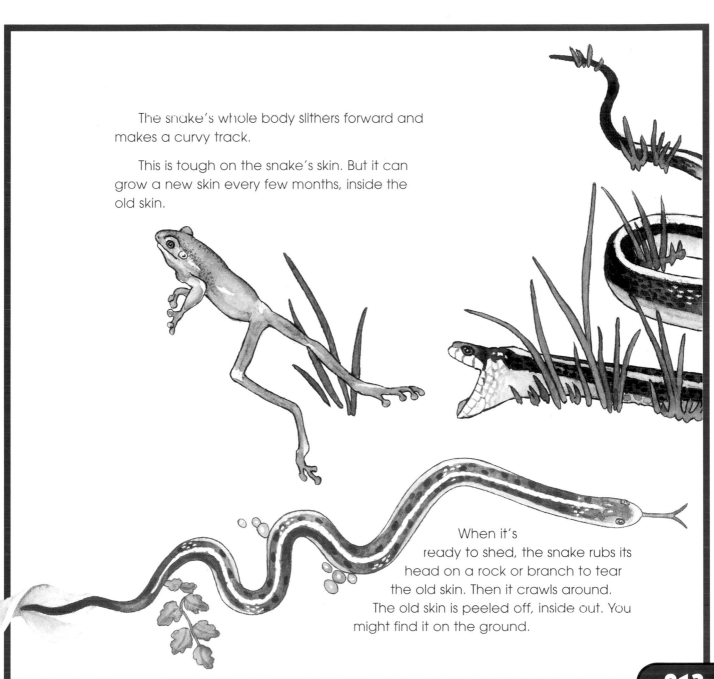

The snake's whole body slithers forward and makes a curvy track.

This is tough on the snake's skin. But it can grow a new skin every few months, inside the old skin.

When it's ready to shed, the snake rubs its head on a rock or branch to tear the old skin. Then it crawls around. The old skin is peeled off, inside out. You might find it on the ground.

BADGERS

Here's a great dirt-digger.
A badger can dig faster than a human
with a shovel. It tears many rough
holes in the ground, hunting for mice
or prairie dogs that live underground.

A badger also digs tunnels and
underground rooms for its own home.
The "front door" hole on top is big.

Badger tracks have five
toes and claw dots—like a
skunk's but bigger. Badger
scat may be full of fur and
little bones.

WALK LIKE THE ANIMALS

Groups of tracks are great clues. Try making different track patterns yourself on a snowy field—or a vacant lot, golf course, or football field. Take along a tape measure.

STRIDE

The distance between footprints is called the "stride." Walk slowly across the snow. Measure the distance between your tracks, from one toe tip to the next. Now try running. Your stride changed a lot—it got longer.

Stride is a clue about how big an animal is. A muskrat's stride is about 4 or 5 inches. A moose's stride may be 3 feet or more.

HOPPING

You can hop with two feet. Rabbits, squirrels, and mice hop with four feet. The front feet land first. Then the back feet come down in front of the front feet. Put your hands down and try to hop that way.

How far can you hop? A mouse usually hops a few inches. A jackrabbit can hop 10 feet or more.

TIGHTROPE WALKING

Foxes and coyotes often walk in a very straight line. Walk across the snow as if you were walking on a tightrope. Keep your tracks in one line.

Foxes and coyotes do this with four feet. The back feet step right on top of the front foot tracks. Bend over and walk on your hands and feet. Try to copy the straight line of fox and coyote tracks.

THE POND

A pond or lake is a natural gathering place. Some animals live in the water. Others visit the pond to drink the water and eat the pond plants and animals.

Look at the mud along the shore for tracks. Some trails may lead away from the pond into a forest or field nearby.

Look at the plants near the shore. They may have been nibbled by ducks or insects. There may be bird nests hidden in the reeds. Dried skeletons of dragonflies may be stuck to the stems. You may see frog or fish eggs in the shallow water.

DUCKS

When a duck paddles across a pond, its webbed feet push the water like a diver's rubber flippers. When it walks on land, it waddles. You can see three straight toes in each footprint. You can often see the web of skin stretched between the toes.

A mother duck hides her nest in the reeds or grass at the edge of the pond. The nest is made of grass and some of her own soft down feathers. She lays her eggs there.

When the fluffy ducklings are strong enough to walk, they follow their mother to the water. Then you'll see big and little tracks together.

RACCOONS

The first raccoon sign you find may be garbage pulled out of a trash can. Raccoons often visit campgrounds and houses. They eat almost anything.

They eat plenty of pond food, too, and leave their own "trash" as clues. They drop crayfish claws and empty turtle shells. They make holes in the ground when they dig up turtle eggs. They tear up duck nests and scatter the empty eggshell halves.

Raccoons walk many miles around ponds and rivers, summer and winter. The tracks look like little hands. A raccoon's front feet work like hands. Its quick fingers can catch fish or frogs or crayfish under water.

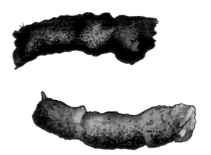

MINKS

If you smell a stink near water, think mink. This little hunter has a smell a bit different from a skunk's, but just as strong.

Minks make tracks along the edges of ponds, streams, and swamps. That's where they hunt for their meals. They eat muskrats, mice, fish, frogs, birds, worms, and insects.

Minks leave twisty, black scats on rocks and logs.

When it snows, minks play!

They slide down hills, sometimes right into an icy stream.
The slide marks are as wide as your hand. They also dive
into the snow, "swim" through it, and pop up
several feet away. You may see the dive
holes near their tracks.

MUSKRATS

When this fat rat runs around a pond, it makes hand-like footprints. Sometimes its skinny tail drags in the mud or snow, making curvy lines.

Muskrats pile up pond plants and sticks to make a lodge. Lodges are built out in a shallow pond or lake, or on the shore. Muskrats eat a lot of plants, and leave piles of plant stalks lying on the bank or on the water.

They munch clams and drop the clamshells. They leave peanut-size droppings on rocks or logs.

In the winter, muskrats make little huts for safe snacking. They collect plants and mud from the bottom of the pond. Next, they push it up through a hole in the ice, and make the roof for the hut. Then, they swim back under the ice to find food, and pop up into the hut to eat it.

TURTLES

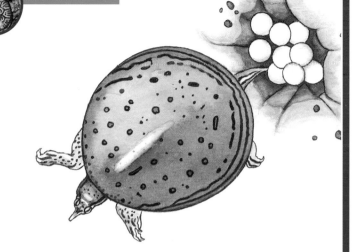

If you see a straight stripe in the mud, with footprints on both sides, it's probably a turtle track. A turtle's stomach is close to the ground. If the shell drags on the ground, it makes a wide stripe. Sometimes only the tail drags, making a thin stripe.

In the summer a mother turtle lays her eggs in the ground. She digs a hole, lays the eggs inside, and covers them with dirt or sand. She may smooth the sand to hide the nest. Many raccoons, skunks, and bears can find it anyway, and eat the eggs. If you find a turtle nest, it's best to leave it alone.

223

FROGS

The long back legs of a frog are great for leaping.
When a frog is hopping across the mud, it lands
with four footprints in a clump—
two large and two small.

The big back feet are like swimming flippers.
The front feet are much smaller, with four tiny toes.

In the spring a female frog lays eggs in the water at the edge of the pond. Each black and white egg, about the size of a peppercorn, is wrapped in a clear jelly coat.

You may find thousands of eggs in a gooey blob, clinging to the pond plants. Later on, tadpoles with tails hatch out of the eggs, and swim in the pond.

BEAVERS

Using its front teeth, a beaver can chop down a tree in three minutes!
Pointy-top tree stumps tell you a beaver pond is nearby.

Beavers can make their own ponds by building a dam across a stream with
logs and mud. You can see trails where the
beavers dragged logs. A wide zigzag
in the mud shows where a
beaver's fat tail was dragging.

Beavers also pile up sticks and mud to make their lodge. The "doors" are hidden under water.

When a beaver eats, it twirls a branch in its paws like corn on the cob. It gobbles the twigs, leaves, and bark. Then it weaves the bare branch into the dam or lodge.

Beavers keep busy all winter. You can see log-drag trails in the snow, or a pile of branches sticking out of the icy pond.

After many years the beavers move away. If the old dam breaks, the water rushes out. Then a meadow grows where the pond was. But you can still see the dam and lodge poking through the grass.

MAKE TRACKS THAT LAST

Animal tracks are just holes in the ground, but you can collect them with this trick. You can fill the tracks with liquid plaster, let it harden, and take the hard "casts" home. They look just like the bottoms of animal feet. This works best for tracks in mud or soft dirt.

HERE IS WHAT YOU WILL NEED

- plaster of Paris powder—in a plastic tub or coffee can with lid
- water—in a water bottle or canteen
- 1 cup measure for plaster powder
- 1/2 cup measure for water
- container to mix plaster in
- spoon
- pocket knife or table knife
- small box

HERE IS HOW TO MAKE THE PLASTER CASTS

1 Find some tracks first. Pick out two or three of the best ones.

2 Put 1/2 cup water in the mixing container.

3 Pour 1 cup plaster powder into the water.

4 Stir with the spoon until the lumps are gone. The plaster should be about as thick as pancake batter or applesauce.

5 QUICKLY pour the plaster into the tracks. Make sure it fills up all the toe holes and claw marks.

6 Let the plaster harden at least 20 to 40 minutes, until it feels as hard as a rock. Look around for more signs while you wait.

7 The casts are still fragile. Carefully cut the dirt around them with the knife, and lift them up gently.

8 Put the casts in the box to protect them on the way home. They will get harder after several hours. You can then rinse the dirt off in the sink. A soft toothbrush helps.

SCRAPBOOK

Tracks, Scats and Signs

Trees, Leaves and Bark

by Diane L. Burns illustrations by Linda Garrow

INTRODUCTION

There are many kinds of trees all around us. They come in many sizes and shapes. This Take-Along Guide and its activities will help you know some of the trees that grow in prairies, woodlands, swamps and mountains across the United States.

TREES HAVE THREE PARTS

THE CROWN is the top of the tree where the branches, leaves, seeds and flowers are found.

THE TRUNK is the stem of the tree covered with bark to protect it. It holds the branches toward the sunlight. And it helps food travel between the roots and the branches.

THE ROOTS are the "underground branches" that pull up water and food for the tree from the soil. Roots hold the tree in place.

TREES CAN BE DIVIDED INTO TWO GROUPS

BROADLEAF trees have leaves that turn color and drop off for the winter. Their seeds grow inside fruits, nuts, pods or berries.

EVERGREEN or conifer trees have needles that stay green all year long. The seeds grow inside cones.

Have fun exploring and learning about Trees, Leaves and Bark.

ASPEN

TIPS TO FIND THIS TREE

Aspen seeds need sunlight to sprout; look for aspens in open areas.

They are the first broadleaf trees to spring up where land has been disturbed.

Listen for the leaves rustling in the breeze.

Aspens grow on open slopes of mountains.

LIFESPAN AND USES

Aspens grow to about 60 feet tall.

The wood is very soft. It makes good newspaper.

Aspens grow fast but only live about 60 years.

INTERESTING FACTS ABOUT ASPEN

Native Americans called this tree "noisy leaf."

Beavers love to eat aspen bark.

Bigtooth aspen and quaking aspen are the two kinds of aspen trees.

They grow throughout New England, the midwestern and western United States.

LEAVES

Aspen leaves are shiny and toothed. They are about the size of a silver dollar.

The leaf stems are flat.

On a branch, aspen leaves alternate like the teeth of a zipper.

BARK

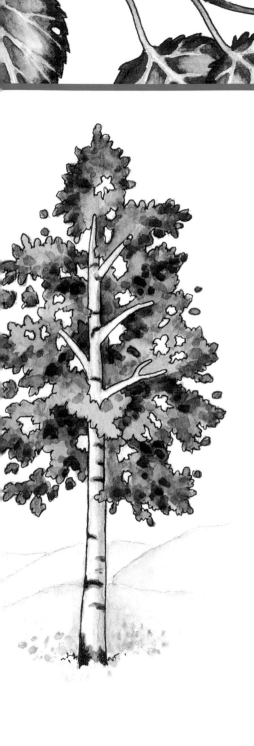

Young aspen trees have smooth, pale green-white bark that looks shiny.

Full-grown trees have darker and rougher bark.

SEEDS

Caterpillar-like flowers become small hairy seeds.

The seeds blow away on the wind.

Tell someone where you are going and how long you will be gone.

WILLOW

TIPS TO FIND THIS TREE

Willows like it when their roots are wet. Look for willows along riverbanks and other wet edges.

In summer, look at the outline of the whole tree. Willow branches often bend toward the ground and wave gracefully in the breeze.

LIFESPAN AND USES

The willow is a short, sturdy tree that grows to 30-60 feet tall.

Willows are planted to keep soil from washing away; the tough roots hold soil against flooding.

Willow wood is soft and bends easily; it makes good toy whistles.

Willows live about 60 years.

INTERESTING FACTS ABOUT WILLOW

Willow bark can be made into aspirin.

There are 80 kinds of American willows. At least one kind grows in each of the 50 states.

LEAVES

Willow leaves are narrow and long, like green fingers.

Each leaf is 3-6 inches long, and they alternate along the branch like teeth of a zipper.

BARK

On young trees, willow bark is smooth and varies from red-brown to green-brown in color.

Grown trees have dark brown bark that is rough and has ridges.

SEEDS

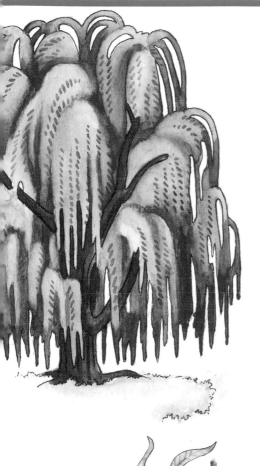

Willow seeds are tiny, like poppy seeds.

These trees grow most easily from pieces of fallen twigs. New trees start wherever the twig lands.

Please treat all trees gently.

COTTONWOOD

TIPS TO FIND THIS TREE

Cottonwoods need sunlight to sprout. Look for them in open areas.

They also grow in dry areas anywhere water is found. Look along streams and creek bottomlands.

Sometimes, cottonwoods are planted for shade and windbreaks. You'll find them near farm and ranch houses.

In summer, use your ears to find cottonwoods. Listen for the rustling of the leaves.

LIFESPAN AND USES

Cottonwoods grow to about 100 feet tall.

The soft wood is made into newspaper.

The trees live more than 100 years.

INTERESTING FACTS ABOUT COTTONWOOD

Bees use the buds' sticky gum to seal cracks in their hives.

There are about a dozen types of cotton-woods in the United States. They grow across New England, the midwestern and western United States.

LEAVES

The shiny green, triangular leaves are 4-7 inches long.

Toothed cottonwood leaves have flat leaf stems.

The leaves alternate along the branch like the teeth of a zipper.

BARK

The bark is thin, smooth and pale gray on young trees.

Older cottonwood bark is dark gray with deep, rounded ridges.

SEEDS

Cottonwoods have male and female trees.

On female trees, seed pods hang from strings. The ripe pods burst open with white fluffy "cotton."

Male cottonwoods have red, ropey flowers that look like fat caterpillars.

Don't hurt any part of a tree with your hands or tools.

JUNIPER

TIPS TO FIND THIS TREE

A juniper can be a scrubby, spreading tree. It can look like a low, prickly bush.

Junipers grow in soil with lots of rocks and sand.

Look in dry areas, too, where other trees cannot grow.

LIFESPAN AND USES

Junipers can grow up to 60 feet tall, but most are much shorter.

Its wood makes good campfires.

The berries are an important food for birds like waxwings, warblers and robins.

Junipers can live 300 years.

INTERESTING FACTS ABOUT JUNIPER

Native Americans used crushed juniper berries as an insect repellent.

There are more than a dozen kinds of junipers in the United States. They grow in the northeastern states, and also from Texas into the southwestern states and north into the Rocky Mountains.

LEAVES

Juniper leaves look like skinny green needles.

The leaves are small (less than half an inch long).

They lay flat against the twig and are rounded and scaly.

BARK

Often thin, scaly red-brown and rough, juniper bark feels shredded and soft.

SEEDS

Juniper seeds are hidden inside bluish berry-cones that are about the size of a pea.

Don't step on saplings
or bend them.

PAPER BIRCH

TIPS TO FIND THIS TREE

Look for the white bark of the trunk in the woods.

Paper Birches often grow in clumps of two or three trees.

In autumn, birch leaves turn bright yellow.

▶ DO NOT PEEL THE RAGGED BARK! It does not grow back.

LIFESPAN AND USES

Paper Birch trees grow quickly to their 60 foot height.

Birch wood is often used to make wooden spoons. It also makes a good campfire because it crackles as it burns, and it smells good.

To add beauty, birches are often planted in yards and town parks.

They live about 60 years.

INTERESTING FACTS ABOUT PAPER BIRCH

Paper Birch is nicknamed "canoe birch" because canoe frames were once covered with the tough, lightweight bark.

About a half-dozen kinds of birch trees grow in the northern United States, from coast to coast.

LEAVES

Birch leaves are egg-shaped, about 3 inches long.

They have pointed tips and thick teeth along the edge.

The leaves feel coarse.

Along the branch, the leaves alternate like the teeth of a zipper.

BARK

Paper Birch bark is smooth, chalk-white, and streaked with black.

The paper-thin bark may hang raggedly from the tree.

The inner bark is orange.

SEEDS

Many tiny winged seeds grow inside a narrow cone.

The cone is about as long as your thumb.

The seeds scatter on the winter winds.

Be aware of everything around you, especially changing weather.

SHAGBARK HICKORY

TIPS TO FIND THIS TREE

Hickories and oaks often grow next to each other.

Shagbark Hickory seeds need shade to sprout.

They grow up under other trees, never by themselves in an open field.

The leaves turn deep yellow in autumn.

LIFESPAN AND USES

Shagbark Hickories grow to be 100 feet tall.

Hard hickory wood makes strong handles for hammers and shovels, and dogsled runners.

Hickory nuts are an important wildlife food for squirrels and deer.

Hickory trees live about 250 years.

INTERESTING FACTS ABOUT SHAGBARK HICKORY

Small, tasty hickory nuts (about 100 to a pound) were important in Early American cooking.

Pioneers made a green dye for clothing from the bark.

The trees grow across the eastern half of the United States.

LEAVES

Shagbark Hickory leaflets are dark yellow-green and about 1 foot long.

They feel hairy on the edges.

There are 5 or 7 leaflets on a leaf. The end leaflet is larger than the others.

BARK

It is gray, and hangs in strips from the trunk.

It looks "shaggy," giving the tree its name.

SEEDS

These are nuts as small as your thumbnail.

They are hidden inside a thick, green husk.

Don't peel the bark, because that hurts the tree's growth.

MAPLE

TIPS TO FIND THIS TREE

Maples like moist, rich woods.

The seeds need shade to sprout.

In summer, look for the winged seeds that twirl to the ground.

In autumn, maple leaves turn shades of bright red and orange-yellow.

Maples are often planted for shade along city streets, in yards and town parks.

LIFESPAN AND USES

Maples grow to about 60 feet tall.

The wood of the maple tree is hard and tough. It makes good flooring for school gyms, and bowling pins.

Maples can live for 300 years or more.

INTERESTING FACTS ABOUT MAPLE

Maple leaves can be up to a foot long and wide.

Sap, a clear liquid that carries food up and down the trunk, can be boiled into maple syrup each spring.

One of a dozen kinds of maples can be found almost anywhere in the United States.

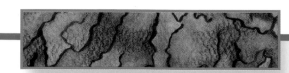

LEAVES

Maple leaves are hand-shaped, about as wide as they are tall.

The leaves grow opposite each other on the branch—"eye to eye."

BARK

Maple bark is silvery and smooth on young trees.

It is dark gray-brown with flaky grooves on older trees.

SEEDS

Maple seeds are winged, and look like the blades of a helicopter.

They drop off the tree in summer.

Don't put your hand into a hole or crack in the tree. It may be an animal's home.

OAK

TIPS TO FIND THIS TREE

Oaks grow almost anywhere, some on drier ground, some on wetter.

In autumn, squirrels and blue jays are busy gathering oak nuts.

In winter, a few leaves cling to most oak branches and rattle in the wind.

LIFESPAN AND USES

Oaks grow from about 20-130 feet tall.

The beautiful, hard wood makes long-lasting furniture, like tables and chairs.

Acorns are important food for wild animals such as squirrels, raccoons and blue jays.

Oaks live from 200-500 years.

INTERESTING FACTS ABOUT OAK

Oak trees are divided into two groups, white oaks and black oaks.

Long ago, white oak nuts were ground into flour by Native Americans. Black oak nuts were too bitter.

A fully grown oak can make 50,000 acorns in one season. They would weigh a half ton!

Oaks grow all across the United States.

Don't leave behind any litter.

LEAVES

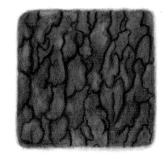

Oak leaves are taller than they are wide.

They have a leathery feel.

They have uneven shapes.

White oak leaves have rounded edges without teeth.

Black oak leaves have pointed edges and bristly teeth.

BARK

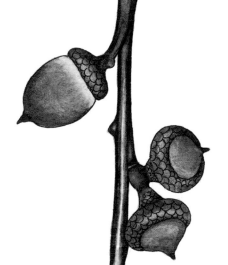

Oak bark is deeply ridged or flaky.

It can be gray-brown to dark brown in color.

SEEDS

Oak seeds are called acorns.

Acorns are brown, roundish nuts set inside a saucer-shaped cup.

EASTERN WHITE PINE

TIPS TO FIND THIS TREE

This pine grows on sandy, well-drained land.

The treetops have a soft, bushy look— like feathers.

► SPECIAL WARNING: Pitch on white pine cones and bark is sticky! It is hard to wash off hands and clothes

LIFESPAN AND USES

Eastern White Pines grow more than 100 feet tall.

The wood is often used for building houses.

These trees live about 400 years.

INTERESTING FACTS ABOUT EASTERN WHITE PINE

Pines are the largest group of conifers.

Long ago, Native Americans boiled white pine needles into a tea that soothed sore throats.

The Eastern White Pine is found throughout New England, southward into Virginia, North Carolina and Tennessee, then westward across the upper midwestern United States.

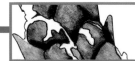

LEAVES

The soft, blue-green needles are about 4 inches long.

They grow in bundles of 5 needles.

BARK

Eastern White Pine bark is thin, smooth and green-gray on young trees.

It is thick, gray-brown and deeply grooved on older trees.

SEEDS

The cones are long and narrow, about 4-6 inches.

They are light brown and papery-feeling.

Globs of sticky pitch cling to the cones.

Stay away from poison ivy and poison oak.

MAKE A LEAF MOBILE

Use leaves from different trees for an interesting mobile.

THINGS YOU WILL NEED

▼

- assorted leaves (choose flat ones for the best results)
- 1 yard of clear contact paper
- 2 yards of thread, cut into 8 inch lengths
- 2 feet of yarn
- 1 toothpick
- 1 sturdy fallen branch about 12 inches long
- 1 pair of scissors
- clear tape

HERE'S HOW

▼

1 Cut two pieces of clear contact paper for each leaf. Make them a little larger than the leaf.

2 Peel the paper from the contact paper. Carefully lay each leaf onto the sticky side and cover it with another piece of peeled contact paper, sticky side down. Smooth out any air bubbles. Trim around the edges, using a scissors.

3 Poke a small hole near the top of each leaf, using the toothpick (but not too close to the top of the leaf or it will tear).

4 Pull a piece of thread through each hole.

5 Tie each leaf to the branch, anywhere. Tape in place.

6 Tie the yarn near the middle of the branch so that the mobile hangs straight and balanced.

Hang the leaf mobile from a hook in your ceiling.

MAKE A PINECONE SNACKBAR FOR BIRDS

Choose your pinecone on a dry day, or bring a wet cone inside
and let it dry out before beginning.

THINGS YOU WILL NEED

- 1 large, open pinecone
- 3 tablespoons of peanut butter
- 2 tablespoons of birdseed
- 1 tablespoon of ground-up bread crumbs
- 1 foot-long piece of thin wire bent into a hook at each end
- 1 sheet of newspaper
- 1 paper napkin

In dry weather, the scales open to release the seeds. In damp weather, the scales close to keep the seeds dry. To make this snackbar, the scales must be open.

HERE'S HOW

1 Spread the newspaper over your workspace to catch any spills.

2 Smear peanut butter over the pinecone's edges and into its cracks, using your fingers. Wipe your hands clean on the napkin.

3 Sprinkle birdseed and bread crumbs over the peanut butter, pressing to keep it in place.

4 Loop the hooked end of the wire around the top of the pinecone, twisting it tightly so it won't come loose.

5 Hang the snackbar on a branch outside.

Then, watch from indoors as the birds enjoy your feast.

AMERICAN SYCAMORE

TIPS TO FIND THIS TREE

Sycamores need much moisture.

Look for them in wet bottomlands.

Watch for the white, patchy look of the trunk.

Sycamore crowns are round and wide.

LIFESPAN AND USES

American Sycamore trees grow to about 100 feet tall.

Its wood makes boxes for shipping things like fruits and vegetables.

The sycamore lives about 500 years.

INTERESTING FACTS ABOUT AMERICAN SYCAMORE

American Sycamores are native to the United States. They grow in the eastern part, and in the streambanks and valleys of the south-western states.

Sycamores grow the widest trunks of any American tree: up to 14 feet!

LEAVES

Sycamore leaves are big—up to 10 inches wide.

Each leaf has 3-5 lobes. The undersides are hairy.

Each leaf is shiny green on top and pale green underneath.

BARK

The sycamore's flat gray bark does not stretch as the trunk grows.

Patches of bark peel off and leave behind bare, white spots.

SEEDS

A solid, spiky-looking ball covers the seeds.

It hangs on the tree all winter.

It is about the size of a golfball.

Don't approach or touch any plants you don't know.

ASH

TIPS TO FIND THIS TREE

Most ash trees in the eastern United States grow in moist places.

Ash seeds drop off in late autumn.

The crown is tall and oval.

LIFESPAN AND USES

Ash trees grow to about 70 feet tall.

Strong, springy ash wood makes sporting goods such as baseball bats and snowshoes.

Ash trees live about 100 years.

INTERESTING FACTS ABOUT ASH

It was once believed that ash trees cured sick children when they passed under the branches.

More than a dozen kinds of ash trees grow in the United States. They are found from the east coast, into the southern states and across the plains states.

LEAVES

These leaves have 7 or 9 leaflets with a few blunt teeth along the edges.

The leaflets are about 10 inches long.

The leaves grow in opposite pairs along the branch.

BARK

Ash bark is grayish.

Its ridges form a diamond shape.

SEEDS

The seeds have slender wings like the blades of a helicopter.

They droop in clusters about 2 inches long.

Don't push against dead tree trunks. They can snap off and hurt you.

EASTERN LARCH

TIPS TO FIND THIS TREE

Wear boots! The larch grows on wet, swampy ground.

Eastern Larches are easiest to find in autumn when their needles turn a soft yellow color.

They often grow close together with slender trunks and skinny branches.

LIFESPAN AND USES

Larches are straight trees that may grow to 60-75 feet tall.

Its wood is used to make newspaper and fenceposts.

A larch may live to be 200 years old.

INTERESTING FACTS ABOUT EASTERN LARCH

Unlike other conifers, the eastern larch sheds its needles each fall.

Larches grow from the Ohio River Valley north all the way to the Arctic, where a fully grown tree may be only several feet tall.

"Tamarack" is a Native American name for the larch.

LEAVES

Larches have soft needles about an inch long.

They grow in bundles of about a dozen needles.

BARK

Eastern Larch bark is scaly and rough.

It is red-brown in color.

SEEDS

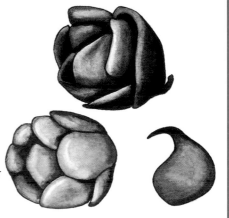

Seeds of the larch tree grow inside small, round cones.

The cones, less than 1 inch long, face upward on the branches.

New cones are greenish and grow at the tip of the branch.

Old cones are brown and grow farther back on the branch.

Don't approach or touch any wild animals you might see.

NORTHERN WHITE-CEDAR

TIPS TO FIND THIS TREE

This tree likes wet places.

It often grows by itself.

It has a compact, triangular shape.

LIFESPAN AND USES

Northern White-cedar grows to about 50 feet tall.

The wood does not rot, so it is used for making roof shingles.

White-cedar is also an important deer food in winter.

These trees live more than 300 years.

INTERESTING FACTS ABOUT NORTHERN WHITE-CEDAR

This tree is also known as Arbor Vitae, which means "tree of life."

It was probably the first American tree carried back to Europe by French explorers.

Northern White-cedar grows in the very northeastern states, into the Great Lakes region, and Virginia, North Carolina and Tennessee.

LEAVES

White-cedar leaves are scale-like and lay flat along the branch.

They are about one-quarter inch long.

They are smooth and dull green.

BARK

White-cedar bark is thin, and gray to red-brown.

It hangs in soft, skinny shredded strips.

SEEDS

White-cedar cones are small, less than one-half inch long.

They are yellow-brown and egg-shaped.

The cones hang either in clusters or alone.

Get permission before going onto someone's land.

LODGEPOLE PINE

TIPS TO FIND THIS TREE

The tree grows slender, leggy trunks on lower ground.

High on the mountain, weather twists and bends its shape.

LIFESPAN AND USES

Lodgepole Pines can grow to about 70 feet tall.

The wood is used for rustic fenceposts around homes and corrals.

This tree lives about 250 years.

INTERESTING FACTS ABOUT LODGEPOLE PINE

The lodgepole pine's slender trunks were used as frames for Native American lodges. The tree was named after them.

Lodgepoles grow from sea level to mountaintop in the western states.

LEAVES

Lodgepole needles are about 2 inches long.

They grow in pairs and look twisted.

They are bright yellow-green.

BARK

Lodgepole bark is pale brown and only about 1 inch thick.

It is made of thin, small scales.

SEEDS

Lodgepole seeds grow inside cones that are shiny yellow-brown.

The cones are less than 2 inches long and grow in clusters.

On the cones, each scale has a slender prickle.

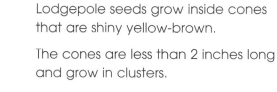

Watch where you step.

PONDEROSA PINE

TIPS TO FIND THIS TREE

Look for the red-orange bark.

Ponderosa Pines have a narrow, tall shape.

They have a feathery-soft look at the top.

LIFESPAN AND USES

They grow to about 200 feet tall.

Ponderosa Pine wood is used to make parts of houses, like the window frames.

Ponderosa Pine trees live as long as 500 years.

INTERESTING FACTS ABOUT PONDEROSA PINE

Ponderosa Pine is also known as Western Yellow Pine.

Explorers Lewis and Clark wrote about it in 1804 on their famous journey out West.

The name "ponderosa" means "massive."

Ponderosa Pines grow on dry uplands of the western and southwestern United States and the plains states.

LEAVES

Yellow-green ponderosa pine needles grow in bundles of 2 or 3.

They are 4-11 inches long.

BARK

Trees younger than 100 years have bark that is nearly black in color.

Trees older than 100 years have bright red-orange bark.

It is formed in large flaky plates with black lines in between.

The flaky plates look like puzzle pieces.

SEEDS

Ponderosa seeds grow inside cones that are 3-5 inches long.

The cones have a prickly hook on each scale.

First-year cones are green. They sit upright on the branch.

Second-year cones turn brown and hang down to spill the seeds.

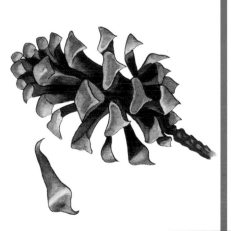

Wear boots and other appropriate clothing.

DOUGLAS FIR

TIPS TO FIND THIS TREE

The treetops have a pointy shape.

Look for the deep grooves in the bark.

INTERESTING FACTS ABOUT DOUGLAS FIR

The bark on these fully grown trees can be a foot thick!

Next to the redwoods, Douglas Fir is the tallest tree in the United States.

Douglas Fir trees grow throughout the western and southwestern United States on drier uplands from sea level up to 9,000 feet.

LIFESPAN AND USES

Douglas Fir trees can grow to 300 feet tall.

The strong wood is used for building houses.

Young trees make very good Christmas trees.

Douglas Fir trees can live for more than 1,000 years!

Take your time and don't hurry.

LEAVES

The flat, short needles are about 1 inch long.

The single needles grow all around the branch.

The needles are dark green in color.

BARK

Douglas Fir bark is thick and red-brown.

It has deep grooves.

SEEDS

Douglas Fir cones hang down.

The cones are reddish and 2-4 inches long.

The cones have three-pronged "tongues" that stick out between the scales.

GROW YOUR OWN TREE

In spring, summer, or autumn, you can plant the young tree outside.

THINGS YOU WILL NEED

▼

- Any closed pine cone, dark in color
- 2 clean, empty 8-ounce yogurt cartons with drain holes poked in the bottom and filled with good garden soil
- 2 waterproof saucers
- 1 paper plate

HERE'S HOW

▼

1 Keep the closed pinecone in a warm, dry place until it opens.

2 Shake the seeds from the pinecone over the paper plate.

3 Choose 2 seeds that are dark in color. (Light-colored seeds will not grow).

4 Plant each of the seeds in its own yogurt cup by pressing lightly into the soil so it is covered.

5 Put the cup on a waterproof saucer in a sunny place.

6 Every few days, water the cup carefully so that the soil is moist, not soggy.

Be sure to leave room around the tree so it isn't crowded.

Water it when it gets dry.

Be patient! Trees grow very slowly.

MAKE A BARK RUBBING POSTER

To make a "bark art" collection, use rubbings from several different trees.

THINGS YOU WILL NEED

▼

- Thin drawing paper, such as onion skin or tracing paper
- 4 thumbtacks
- Assorted crayon stubs with the paper peeled off
- Any mature trees with healthy bark

HERE'S HOW

1 Use thumbtacks to pin a piece of paper against the tree trunk at eye level.

2 Rub the flat length of the crayon across the paper.

3 Change the crayon color as often as you like.

4 As you rub, the pattern of the bark will appear.

5 Hang your poster where everyone can admire it.

Bark can be hurt, so thumbtack your paper just deep enough to hold it in place.

When you are done, be sure to remove the thumb-tacks and take them home with you.

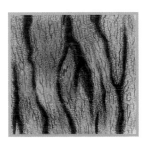

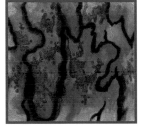

SCRAPBOOK
Trees, Leaves and Bark